TEX FILES

# TEX FILES

ISSUE 01: Towards Architecture

@ The University of Texas at Arlington

Published by
University of Texas at Arlington
School of Architecture
601 Nedderman Drive, Suite 203
Arlington, Texas 76019

www.uta.edu/architecture

Copyright © 2004

Karen Bullis. Editor
Ron Reeves. Art Director
Troy C. Brown, Jason Arndt. Designers
Chuck Pratt. Guest Photographer
Troy C. Brown, David Hook, Ronnie Parsons. Photographers

Special thanks to: Roger Connah, Michael McCarthy, Chris Reeves and all contributing practitioners, professors and students.

TEX FILES is proud to present excerpts of the recently concluded 2002–2003 academic year in a new annual architectural journal. The book serves to document and transcribe a commentary on issues in architecture, education and practice, from the perspective of students, faculty, alumni and professionals. TEX FILES introduces a series of internal and external critical dialogues, archiving, and overall awareness of student work and current architectural events in the greater Dallas, Fort Worth area.

ISBN: 0-9753775-0-7
TEX FILES
ISSUE 01: Towards Architecture

Printed in the United States of America.

# CONTENTS

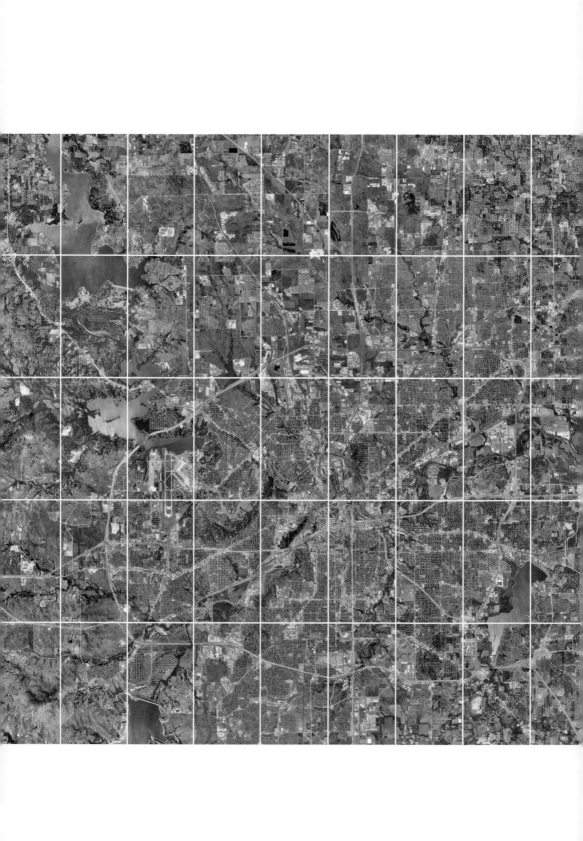

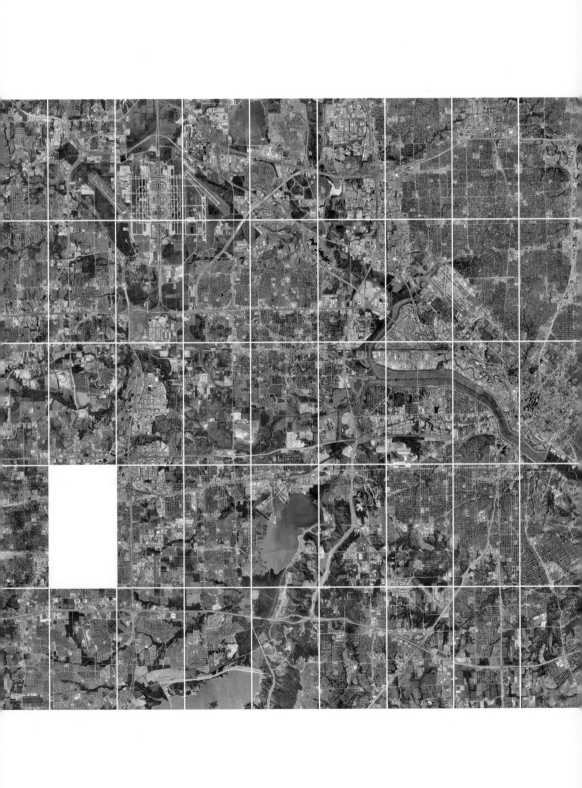

**FACT** Dallas is the ninth largest city in the United States with over one million residents. In Texas Dallas is the third largest city, following Houston and San Antonio. By 2010 the DFW area is expected to rank fourth in the nation in population.

**FACT** Dallas is home of the first shopping mall, Highland Park Village. With more than 36 malls and hundreds of shops and boutiques, Dallas boasts more shopping centers per capita than any other major U.S. city.

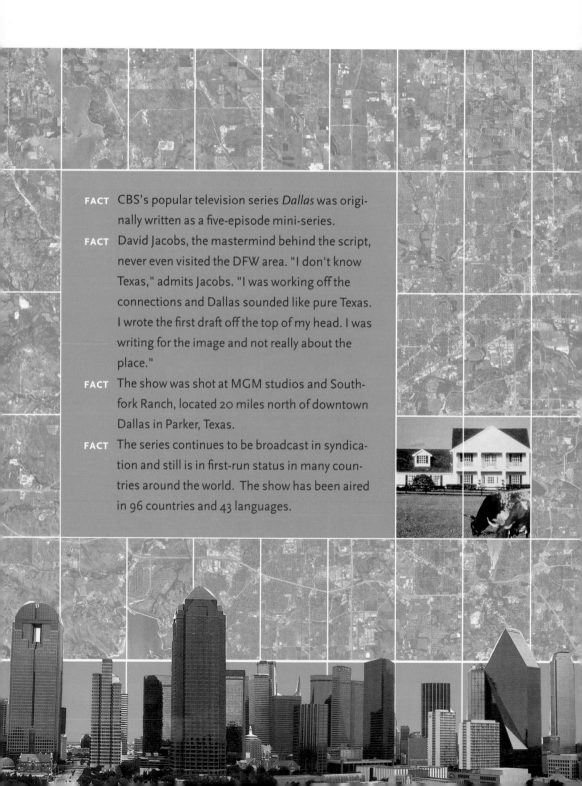

FACT CBS's popular television series *Dallas* was originally written as a five-episode mini-series.

FACT David Jacobs, the mastermind behind the script, never even visited the DFW area. "I don't know Texas," admits Jacobs. "I was working off the connections and Dallas sounded like pure Texas. I wrote the first draft off the top of my head. I was writing for the image and not really about the place."

FACT The show was shot at MGM studios and Southfork Ranch, located 20 miles north of downtown Dallas in Parker, Texas.

FACT The series continues to be broadcast in syndication and still is in first-run status in many countries around the world. The show has been aired in 96 countries and 43 languages.

# DFW FACT/FICTION

Holly Arthur

**12,000 square miles**

**12 counties**

**54 cities** (over 10,000 people)

**5.7 million residents**

**No. 1 destination in Texas**

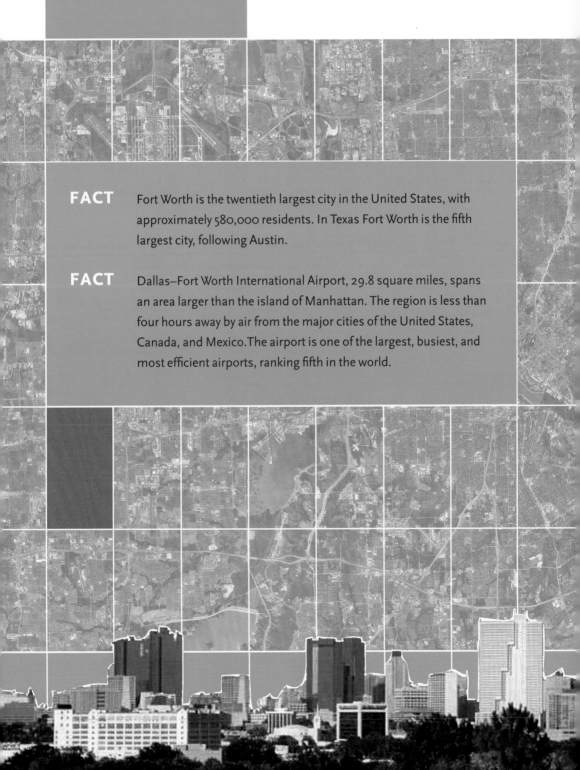

**FACT**    Fort Worth is the twentieth largest city in the United States, with approximately 580,000 residents. In Texas Fort Worth is the fifth largest city, following Austin.

**FACT**    Dallas–Fort Worth International Airport, 29.8 square miles, spans an area larger than the island of Manhattan. The region is less than four hours away by air from the major cities of the United States, Canada, and Mexico. The airport is one of the largest, busiest, and most efficient airports, ranking fifth in the world.

# CONTRIBUTORS

### Dialogue One
**Culture of Speculation**

EDWARD M. BAUM, FAIA is a registered architect, Fellow of the American Institute of Architects, and Professor of Architecture at the University of Texas at Arlington where he joined the faculty as dean in 1988. His professional work has won a number of competitions and awards, most recently an American Architecture Award and a Texas Society of Architects Honor Award for the *Dallas Police Memorial* (with J.P. Maruszczak), and a Texas Society of Architects Honor Award for prototype infill housing in Dallas. He is a founder of the Dallas Architecture Forum.

DIANE CHEATHAM is a Dallas-based real estate developer. She established Urban Edge Developers in 1996 whose properties have been featured in *Texas Architect*, *GA Houses*, *D Home*, *Dallas Life Magazine* and many others. She is currently completing a housing project (with S. Odum) in Knox-Henderson.

GEORGE GINTOLE is Associate Professor of Architecture at UT Arlington and Visiting Professor at the Department of Theoretical and Applied Aesthetics at the University of Lund in Sweden where he has taught workshops in Urban and Industrial Design since 1996. He is co-founder of the multi-media firm The Art of Logic, with Stephen Duck, Boston and is involved in the Book Arts where he lectures and gives workshops in TEXT-based ART. His work is published in *Letter Arts Review*, *Calligraphy Review*, *Texas Architect*, *The Princeton Journal*, *Lotus International*, and *The Education of an Architect II*.

SHARON ODUM, principal of Sharon Odum Architect, lives and works in Dallas, Texas. She received the Dallas American Institute of Architects Citation Award for Unbuilt Projects in 2000 and earned the Dallas AIA Merit Award in 2001. She is the School of Architecture's 2003 Distinguished Alumni and is currently completing a housing project with Urban Edge Developers in Knox-Henderson.

RON WOMMACK, FAIA, principal of Ron Wommack Architect, is a Fellow of the American Institute of Architects and has been recognized by the AIA at state and local levels for his innovative urban housing work in Dallas, Texas. He has taught at UT Arlington in addition to being an active member of the Dallas Chapter AIA. He is the President of the Dallas Architecture Forum.

### Dialogue Two
**Architectural Concrete**

W. MARK GUNDERSON, AIA is an architect in private practice in Fort Worth, Texas. He is a contributing author to the forthcoming book *Buildings of Texas* and has written extensively for *Texas Architect*, *Cite*, and *Competitions*. He is currently serving on the boards of the Dallas Architecture Forum, the Dallas Architectural Foundation and the Advisory Council of the University of Texas at Arlington School of Architecture, where he has taught design studios as a Visiting Critic. In addition he is a past president of the Fort Worth AIA. Gunderson organized and moderated the concrete symposium presented in "Dialogue Two."

FRED LANGFORD worked as an architect with Louis I. Kahn from 1961 to 1966 on the *Olivetti-Underwood Factory* in Harrisburg, Pennsylvania; the *Salk Institute Laboratories* at La Jolla, California; and, the *Second Capital of Pakistan* in Dacca where he worked with local officials to develop the capacity to produce the kind of concrete that Kahn desired for the project. Langford returned to work with Kahn as a consultant for the *Kimbell Art Museum* in Fort Worth, Texas, carrying forward the formwork vocabulary derived at the *Salk*. Since completion of the *Kimbell* and other diverse projects Langford's practice, established in 1967, has focused on water parks and structures.

TOM SEYMOUR was Vice President for Thos. S. Byrne, Inc., the construction company that built the *Kimbell*. He was in charge of the *Kimbell* project and was also instrumental in the construction of the *Amon G. Carter Museum* and the *Water Gardens*. Seymour was the project officer at Byrne for Steven Holl's *Stretto House*, for Antoine Predock's *Rose Residence* and for Richard Meier's *Rachofsky Residence*. He currently serves as a consultant and expert witness in construction-related matters.

PAUL SIPES is a Vice President and Senior Project Manager with Linbeck, Inc. He was the Project Superintendent for the construction of Tadao Ando's *Modern Art Museum* of Fort Worth, Texas. Sipes also worked on the *Bass Performance Hall* in Fort Worth. He has been involved in a number of complex large projects involving concrete work and is presently working in Houston, Texas on a Federal Reserve Bank.

### Dialogue Three
**Edwin Chan Speaks to Students**

EDWIN CHAN is Design Partner at the office of Frank Gehry and Associates. Collaborating with Gehry to provide design leadership, Chan has been responsible for projects including the *Weisman Art Museum* in Minneapolis; the *Nationale-Nederlanden Office Building* in Prague, Czech Republic; the *Guggenheim Museum* in Bilbao, Spain; as well as the *Art of the Motorcycles Exhibitions* for the *Guggenheim Museum* in New York, Bilbao and Las Vegas. Currently under construction are *Marques de Riscal* Winery in Spain and the *Museum Marta* in Hereford, Germany. Chan has recently ventured into the world of set design in collaboration with Academy Awards winning director William Friedkin (*The Exorcist*) for the upcoming operas *Ariadne auf Naxos* by Richard Strauss and *Tannhauser* by Richard Wagner.

MARTIN PRICE is an Architect and Professor of Architecture at UT Arlington. Exhibitions depicting his work and his students' work that resonate with nature as groundscrapers have been presented throughout the United States and in Finland, Norway, Sweden, Denmark, Britain, Poland, and Spain. The work has been published in *Architectural Review*, *L'architettura*, *Inland Architect*, *A+U*, *Arrikitehti*, *Fisuras*, *Architektur + Wettgewerbe*, *Quaderns*, and *Metalocus*.

### Dialogue Four
**One-on-One with Sanford Kwinter**

SANFORD KWINTER is a New York-based writer and designer. He is co-founder and former editor of *Zone* and *Zone Books*, and writes extensively on philosophical issues of design, architecture and urbanism including *Architectures of Time: Toward a Theory of the Event in Modernist Culture*. In addition to teaching at schools throughout the United States and Europe he is Associate Professor of Architecture at Rice University in Houston, Texas.

JANE TEPLITSKAYA is a fourth year architecture student at UT Arlington. She drove to Houston, Texas to interview Sanford Kwinter for a theory paper in Contemporary Architectural Thinkers.

### P.U.L.P.

ROGER CONNAH is a freelance writer, researcher and teacher based in Stockholm and Ruthin, North Wales where he runs *The Hotel Architecture Retreat and Resistance Centre*. His books include: *40 Young Architects from Finland*; *Zahoor ul Akhlaq*; *How Architecture Got its Hump*; *Sa(l)vaged Modernism*; *Welcome to the Hotel Architecture*; *K/K: A Couple of Finns and Some Donald Ducks (Cinema in Society)* and the award winning *Writing Architecture*. Recent projects (with J.P. Maruszczak) include *Chromotopia* (Unbuilt Architecture Award, Boston Society of Architects, 2003); *Interface, Animall and Brautigan* (Finalist, Dead Malls International Competition, L.A. Forum, 2003); *Pulping Detroit*. Forthcoming: *Modern Architectures in History: Finland* and *The Pulp Architecture Manual* (with J.P. Maruszczak).

J.P. MARUSZCZAK is Associate Professor of Architecture at UT Arlington. He has won numerous awards in architectural competitions, including an American Architecture Award and Texas Society of Architects Honor Award for the *Dallas Police Memorial* (with E. Baum). Recent collaborations (with R. Connah) include *Chromotopia*; *Interface, Animall and Brautigan*; and *Pulping Detroit*. His work is published in *Progressive Architecture*, *Princeton Journal*, *Japan Architect*, *Texas Architect*, *Landscape Architecture*, and in *The Education of an Architect*. *P.U.L.P.* is an excerpt from the forthcoming book *The Pulp Architecture Manual* (with R. Connah).

### Guest Contributors

HOLLY R. ARTHUR is a graduate architecture student at UT Arlington. Her "Fact/Fiction" episode is an abstract from a compositional paper she is working on entitled "DFW."

JENNIE MAGANN is a Path A graduate student with an undergraduate education in Historic Preservation. Her recent focus includes studies on architecture and its relation to film. "Observations from an Intern" presented here concerns her current work with Sharon Odum.

JESSIE MARSHALL, DIP. ARCH. (RIBA), is a practicing architect and lecturer in the School of Architecture, UT Arlington. She is a doctoral candidate at the Architectural Association, London and was recently awarded a Fulbright grant to teach and conduct research at the Universidad Católica de Valparaíso in Chile. "The Cultivation of Site" appears in the forthcoming *306090 07: Landscape within Architecture*.

CHUCK PRATT works in 4-D non-sequential, non-linear media, which describes his meander through the Path A graduate program at UT Arlington. The photographs featured in part titles are selections from his *Suburban View* series.

TERESA D. RITTER is a fourth year architecture student at UT Arlington and a recreational photographer. Her photographs in "Dialogue Two" were taken the evening of the Concrete Symposium.

# DEAN'S STATEMENT

You are now holding the latest publication of the School of Architecture—newly christened TEX FILES—and offering a snapshot of the School as it is today. Our last similar publication was over 10 years ago and a new review of the School was long overdue, but all good things take time and commitment to produce and I'm sure you'll think it was worth the wait.

As you might anticipate, much of the space herein is devoted to student projects and I think you will agree with me that it shows some of the truly exemplary work produced in all three of the academic programs: Landscape Architecture, Architecture and Interior Design. In addition, there are a number of other features that merit your extra attention: alumni profiles, faculty projects and some intriguing factoids about the DFW metropolis. In particular, the Dialogues distributed throughout the volume are an insight into the viewpoints of a diverse cross section of practitioners, faculty and theorists on a number of contemporary design issues.

Publications such as these are neither easy nor inexpensive to produce. So I want to particularly thank Assistant Professor Karen Bullis for her commitment to seeing this project through to completion and to also recognize her dedicated team of student assistants—Ron Reeves, Troy C. Brown and Jason Arndt—who did much of the work. I also want to thank the numerous friends, members of local design community and visitors to the School who contributed to the content you will find inside. And finally, if you are as enthusiastic about this edition as I hope you will be, might I suggest you send us a tax deductible donation in support of the next edition of TEX FILES?

Donald Gatzke AIA, Dean
August 2004

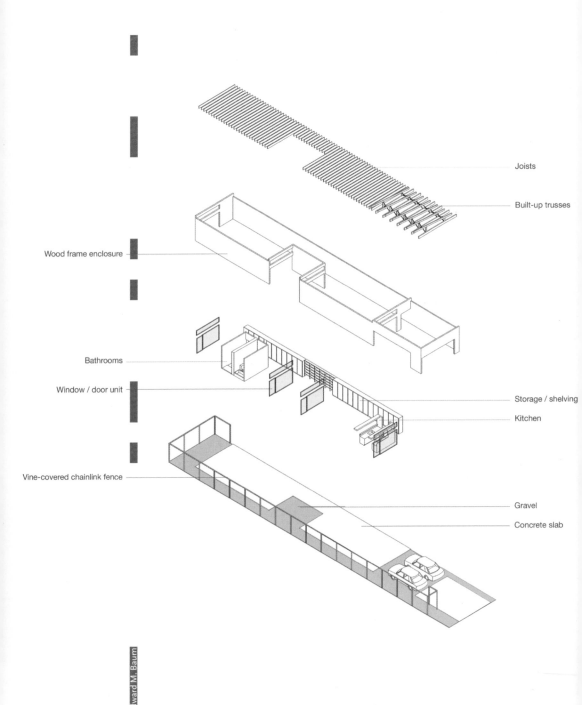

Joists

Built-up trusses

Wood frame enclosure

Bathrooms

Window / door unit

Storage / shelving

Kitchen

Vine-covered chainlink fence

Gravel

Concrete slab

Edward M. Baum

# Dialogue one

## Culture of Speculation
### Housing in DFW

**TEX FILES** The purpose of these dialogues is to document and transcribe a commentary on architecture, education, and practice. We thought it would be fantastic to have a conversation regarding how you have begun to make a difference for housing in Dallas. How do you see your role in redefining or reinventing the nature of housing?

**DIANE CHEATHAM** I take a large risk, a large financial risk doing product. Not so much today because I think our world is finally being sought after. I started doing this in the early 1980s, when truly 75 percent of my clients were gay and the other 25 percent were Jewish.

**EDWARD M. BAUM** With no overlap?

**DIANE CHEATHAM** We didn't go that far. Many of my clients today are empty nesters in their mid-50s, 60s, leaving very traditional houses in the Park Cities. There's been a real shift over the last 25 years. I provide a product out there for someone to see what is available; whereas, most contemporary houses are built by people building houses for themselves. There is very little good speculative work that's done.

**SHARON ODUM** Did you start out wanting to do Modern or Contemporary, or were you guided?

**DIANE CHEATHAM** I had some good counseling from Lionel Morrison. Well, actually I'll take it back to Davis Stocks. When we sold the very traditional house he said come look at this Oglesby condo. We had met Lionel and Susan before and when we moved into that house, they were a lot more excited about doing work together. That is when it started.

**SHARON ODUM** Seeing the Ogelsby space converted you?

**DIANE CHEATHAM** Yes. Like everybody else, you go out and look for houses, look at what's available. You don't know any different. You don't know any better.

**GEORGE GINTOLE** The origins of Modernism were economics. It had a spiritual side to it too, but hygienic. It imparted aspects of cleanliness, purity, unadornment. So there was some aspect too that probably you felt Diane, when you saw that house. Drawings and models are what students see. Often it becomes more of a conceptual issue, but when it is experienced it's transformative. I experienced this and my students experienced this two years ago when I took them to Love Field. There was a hangar for Lear jets. It was the beginning of my methods course and I was interested in product design and industrial design moving away from architecture trying to find ideas outside of it. One student flew to

Houston and they took him to this aircraft carrier hangar. It was all white. It was like one of the churches in Europe, a Baroque church, in terms of its spatiality. It was white floors, white walls, white ceiling, and white jets with the light coming in. It was a beautiful day, one of the hangar doors was open and you could see blue sky. That was a spiritual moment. The problem with Modernism is that it started in war-torn Europe as a way of quickly rebuilding it, and then, as often happens with a lot of movements, you have the frontiers, the people at the forefront, and you have the imitators. The imitators often do more of the lesser quality works.

TEX FILES It began also with a social context that I'm not sure is still with us.

GEORGE GINTOLE The social aspect has shifted now to the entertainment industry and architecture seems to be the stage set.

EDWARD M. BAUM Architecture has shifted to the entertainment business. Architects now have much more celebrity than they ever had before. Someone once defined a celebrity as a person who is famous for being famous. Which is often the case. Their actual achievement is not nearly as much as their notoriety. But the question of the social aspect, Modern architecture can't really be understood without that. It came to America, in some parts thanks to Philip Johnson, distilled of much of the social meaning. In fact he called his exposition International Style—not the International Movement, which was what it was called in Europe. It became a series of formal questions, not social or economic or political questions, and it has remained that way. One of the reasons is that we have essentially completely atomized and privatized the market for housing in America. It's one of the few industries we have which is not consolidated in some way. Unlike manufacturing, finance, or media it's made up of a large number of small actors. It's the only major industry in the country that's that way. So it's very hard to move except by emulation, by copying other things. Better design, or even design of some sort of experimentation, would let the market—if the market had a wider set of choices—start to sort it out. I do believe in the market, but not in a market where the variation runs from A to B of choices. Like cars, if all you had to choose from were American cars, you'd have 20 choices but none of them would be that good. The same thing happens, sort of in spades, in housing. What Diane has done is over the last 20 years introduce us first to VWs, then to Toyotas, and occasionally to a Lexus, where we used to just have Chevys and Fairlanes and Dodge Darts—and still do in most of the alternatives. In Europe a third of the housing is done by the government, called social housing. It's good housing, it's for the middle class, the lower-middle class, and the lower classes. Those are all required to have architects. So all the architects get really heavily tuned up to housing one way or another. The government also insists that housing last a long time because they do not want to invest in something that will self-destruct in five years, so the method of construction is much different. It's meant to be there 25, 30, 50 years from now. We have the real estate and finance interests, which look very suspiciously on any sort of change from the normative and make it very difficult to finance things or even build in some locations unless you conform. These are extremely powerful conservative forces that limit the market. Diane has found, she and Sharon have found, that there is a tremendous market for some alternative at the income level they are aiming at on Cole Avenue. Half of the units were sold before the spade turned. There's a demand out there. This is even an uninformed demand because there was not a lot of publicity on that project.

DIANE CHEATHAM Basically there was none. I sold 10 units before we even put a sign up with our name on it out front.

EDWARD M. BAUM It was a combination of location, design, and strategic price point.

RON WOMMACK To show you how far the market has come, that Parkwood town home project was the first new project at Travis and Buena Vista. The bank would only allow them to build four units initially and required them to put 25 percent of the equity up front. They wouldn't loan them any more money until they sold those four units. The only way they got sold was after they sat there for about four to five months, we finally put furniture in one to show people how to live in it, then the first one sold. Then they moved the furniture to the next one and it sold, and so on. When they went to the bank for the financing on the next eight, the inspector at the bank recommended the bank not give them the loan because in her opinion the units were really cheap. They had no crown moldings, no ornamental metal work or fancy hardware. Finally, the bankers came down for themselves, saw the town homes, and changed their minds. The town homes were being recommended again because they were Modern.

DIANE CHEATHAM The appraisers always have an amazing hand, which is one of the reasons I always use the same appraiser. I go to great lengths with different lenders to get that appraiser approved, because she knows and likes residential. I can look over the history of the Dallas County appraisal district in my Contemporary houses, and older rental houses that I have bought. My Contemporary houses have historically been between 50 and 60 percent of the real value, because the appraisers don't like them.

RON WOMMACK The work that's been going on down there, that is represented by this group, has been about ideas, architectural ideas, and not really stylistic conformity. What you see is just a manifestation of those ideas built in a market pragmatically and priced reasonably. In terms of reinventing or redefining, it is more of a psychological shift. It is also a desire for much more density in places and the ability to own a place rather than just have to rent, which has spawned a lot of work in that area.

**TEX FILES** Since you mentioned the notion of density, I'm curious how that represents an influence on the way you work. Is it important to you? How important is it to this region?

**SHARON ODUM** It's extremely important. We can begin to make our cities much more dense cities. We've begun in the Uptown area or the Knox Street area, and we are expanding out in Mockingbird Station and those areas. I was in Frisco this past weekend, one of the only times I think I've ever been to Frisco. North of somewhere. The sprawl—you just drive and drive and drive and drive and it's the same sprawl. Twenty-five years from now will those be the communities that they think that they'll be? Or will we be in Oklahoma? Or will we all come back to town and have our dense city?

**EDWARD M. BAUM** Developers like density because they get more units per acre.

**DIANE CHEATHAM** The truth is to be in Oak Lawn, you better have density there, because otherwise, your numbers are out of sync. If you don't keep land and building costs reasonably in sync, you just can't play.

**EDWARD M. BAUM** The task for the architect is assuming that density, whatever the density needs to be. How do you make something that's really very livable? And approachable?

**GEORGE GINTOLE** It takes lawmakers. You were talking about the bankers and the appraisers, but then there are the people planning the cities. One city that is desk plotting is Portland, Oregon. They established ring growths, which we have multiple ring growths here. There are disincentives to build outside these ring growths. Architects are teaming up with realtors and developers, scouting the city and finding sites to build. It's all this infill so the city gradually densifies itself.

**SHARON ODUM** My neighborhood group is going through petitioning to change multi-family zoning to town houses because they want to downsize. I have been harassed and harassed and harassed to sign this petition and I refuse to do it. It's ridiculous. Why do we want to downsize? Then you look at the developers who have come to Oak Lawn, who have destroyed Oak Lawn. They need to be strung up by their toes. They've created so much area over there and not made a community and not put anything towards street development. The same species of trees, wouldn't that have been incredible? Something as simple as grass.

**RON WOMMACK** That's a great case where density has held such a high value that it's to the detriment of things. Leave out a unit here and there for the community for some open space.

**TEX FILES** How does the issue of the Metroplex culture play a part in your practice?

**EDWARD M. BAUM** There's the capacity to take risks. When I came here I realized very quickly that I was in the middle of a culture of speculation, not a culture of investment. Investment is putting money down for the future. Somebody told me, "Yes, of course, here in Texas we've been doing that since Texas began. Speculating in land, in cattle, in farm commodities, in oil, in real estate, everything else. We don't manufacture much here. We don't make things here. We don't make *things* we make *deals*." It takes a long time and a different mind-set to deal with investment. It is under the old mainland Protestant ethic that you plant an acorn to make a tree you will never see that will mature long after you are gone. That notion of investing for the long, even intergenerational future which is characteristic of the Protestant ethic is also very conservative because it deals with predictability. Speculation is much more open to what can work now. I find that the acceptance of Modern architecture is really very good here compared to wherever else I've been.

GEORGE GINTOLE But there are cities like Los Angeles and Houston that have done it far longer. The Sun Belt has done a lot of speculation, as well.

EDWARD M. BAUM But those are also cities that started out with speculation. The very positive things here, compared to other places in America, are the acceptance of Modern design, also the sense of emulation. If something's hot in Los Angeles we want it here. If there's a design idea somewhere they are willing to adapt it because of a certain admiration. Now where that admiration comes from we might not want to discuss too far, but it's a fact and a very useful fact for architecture, the sense of the population wanting to try to keep up to date.

RON WOMMACK Yes, Dallas does have opportunities to do Modern work, but it's really been smaller boutique-type projects. When you see what's being done now on Turtle Creek, all the new things that have been announced around the Crescent, it's like Disneyland. When you talk about the major players in multi-family, and they'll tell you, they're just theme architects. That's really what the lion's share—probably 90 percent—of the market is compared to the number of dwelling units. So we really have a small impact.

DIANE CHEATHAM I hadn't noticed a theme yet, but maybe there's one. I drove through yesterday, down Buena Vista and Travis, and it's just amazing. All of it. What were they thinking?

EDWARD M. BAUM It's a kind of drag show. It's architectural drag. It's dolled up without any reference to authenticity, the same way a drag situation is, which is overstated. The building is wearing the equivalent of a feather boa in order to establish a quick, cheap connection, in that case between a gender transfer and here to some other time or other life, heavily filtered through Hollywood. Those images are straight out of the media of the good life and therefore don't have to be very deep because they are very quick takes.

SHARON ODUM Is it Hollywood or Madison Avenue? We are so continually stimulated by advertising images. As a culture we are constantly fed images of comfort and wealth and what it means to be successful and that means buying the French château home.

EDWARD M. BAUM The affectation of the historical is something that the nouveau riche has in every culture; it's not new here. New money always tries to demonstrate a heritage it doesn't have or wish it had. You find these new rich wanting to put up châteaux or castles or palazzi, all these things that allude to a background, to synthesize a background for themselves to gain respectability in some way, not being comfortable with who they are and where they come from.

**RON WOMMACK** I guess that's why I keep going back to concrete block and corrugated metal from west Texas. I fantasize all the time about architecture, fantasies about building incredible mixed-use developments downtown that start to really build a community. We could have a whole range of things for your life, and we would never theoretically have to leave downtown. There is so much vacant land down there and the Europeans have given us so many wonderful typologies to use that are just sitting there waiting to be tapped. Here we only know about the townhouse genre or the multi-family suburban garden apartment—not much in between. Things could be more oriented towards sustainable thinking, more holistic thinking about where we are in this place, related to this weather, winds, basic fundamental stuff that I learned when I was a freshman. In Lubbock they took us out and showed us where the wind came from and we drew these charts with sun angles. The older I get there's more discussion about sustainability. All the LEED [(Leadership in Energy and Environmental Design) Green Building Rating System] stuff has kind of been lip service to that type of thinking. Those are the fundamental ideas that can take housing to a new place that's away from stylistic, shallow issues to more fundamental things about how we live in this place and what resources we have. That's going to take city planning, and that takes city planning on a major scale.

**DIANE CHEATHAM** Why do you think there is lip service to LEED?

**RON WOMMACK** LEED is kind of a transition. If you use a certain kind of toilet or if you use a certain roof color, you get so many points for it. At the end of the day it's politically correct—like the new police station, for instance. It's considered a silver but when you walk down there, what is different about that building from any other building that's being built? Maybe a few subtle things, but not fundamentally—it's not really a green building in my mind. Green thinking is totally radically different thinking about how you get rid of half of this mechanical equipment that's using energy. It's building much more substantial structures that are shading the glass, maybe having less glass. When you see the older structures that have much more substantial walls and are much more thermally stable you don't need much mechanical to heat and cool those. It's a shift, and it's just much more. It's a different kind of thinking than just a checklist. So many buildings around here have west orientations and have so much glass on them it's unbelievable to me, and that's a silver rated building. I don't get that. When we were freshmen in school there was a book by an Arizona professor, Edward Mazria, called *The Passive Solar Energy Book*. It's so wonderful; it is just basic stuff. Then there is Neutra's *Survival Through Design*, which is all about environmental, naturally green, or sustainable thinking.

GEORGE GINTOLE I had a similar reaction. I couldn't understand about the landscape and the climate and the housing. I went to the dean and asked, "Where is the indigenous architecture in this 108-degree heat with wood shingle roofs, and wood construction everywhere?" I thought it would be masonry. I couldn't find courtyard houses, adobe houses, things with shade.

EDWARD M. BAUM The part we are in is really not a part of the Southwest. It is part of the Midwest, geologically, climatically, economically. We are hot and semi-dry. We're in the plains. Being from the Midwest, it all looked pretty familiar, the idea of the dogtrot house, the big porches, and wood architecture. There's a very good reason for it. Wood was cheap, number one. Wood has the capacity to insulate. Wood buildings weather well. You can build them with only two guys. They are easily modified. If the roof is ventilated, the wood shingle roof works perfectly well. It keeps the radiant heat. Wherever there is a place that has a lot of heat you'll see things like overhangs and porches and tall windows and high ceilings. It's not so much of a material response as a volume response.

TEX FILES How do you deal with these site conditions and the sometimes conflicting demands between these conditions, code constraints, clients, masses, concepts, and budget? How do you begin to take all that in when they are sometimes or most of the time conflicting?

SHARON ODUM Ignore it all. Just ignore it all. As one constraint comes you just deal with it. You can't let all that bog you down. You have to go with your first instincts about a project. You've got to get a certain amount of density, a certain amount of units. It's got to cost a certain amount. You've got to make sure it meets all the codes. You may have to get variances. You may have to get whatever—but you just deal with it and those constraints usually bring something out from the architecture. Whether it's a certain setback, you manipulate. You take the code, take the constraint and you try to push it as hard as you can. And out of that comes, hopefully, a good solution that is honest in its response.

RON WOMMACK Actually, I like it when those forces act on a project and make you do something. The project becomes richer because of it. You'll be finished with a scheme essentially and you'll have a curve thrown at you. I used to get kind of pissed off about that because your scheme is already perfect, why is anybody messing with it? But hopefully the more mature you get, you're not as concerned with just the beautiful object but that you're working the process. I love it when something affects it and calls you to do something you wouldn't normally do. Those sorts of things are things you can take to the next project with you. You're looking for one of those influences or forces to affect it.

EDWARD M. BAUM Sharon had it exactly right. You just deal with it. The way you deal with it, if you deal with it well, is to accommodate necessity. All we are talking about is really necessity here, the found situation. The found situation is like the found object in early twentieth century art. You incorporate it. You enhance it, even celebrate it. Art theorists, whomever they are, would have you think, some of them, that the art really exists not in the product but in the bargaining, with the constraints, the negotiation with the world as it is. That's what Christo says about his wrappings. The wrappings aren't the objects of art. The art is all those years of negotiation to be able to get it done. This really is much more how architecture operates, and in particular in this kind of setting. In the case study houses that I just finished I had a window unit and they were all the same so I thought it was really good. Diane said several times, "Ed, those are too damn expensive."

DIANE CHEATHAM Many times.

EDWARD M. BAUM I go through my usual 10 minutes of grumbling. Then I get a back wave of things. Gee, I could do this, this, this, and this. By dealing with it, with what she thought was a strong constraint, I had to come up with something that ended up being far better than anything I had thought of in terms of the window enclosures.

DIANE CHEATHAM That actually happened several times. It was a pattern. I complained a lot, you grumbled about it, and you came back with a much better answer.

EDWARD M. BAUM And I couldn't have come up with that without the push, without it being an irritant.

DIANE CHEATHAM That little change was the difference between making money on that project and not. I think I have had a nice impact in my area. One thing that was said to me a couple of months ago by a realtor, "You know they're selling that project over yada yada, it's just like what Diane Cheatham would do." Well, that's a good thing. Someone is out there trying to hire architects. It's not easy bucking the trends.

RON WOMMACK At the end of the day you always hope that the projects you work on are intelligent. It's about something very simple and maybe a kind of silence about them instead of over-design, just a subtlety and silence, an intelligence about them.

GEORGE GINTOLE The issue of authenticity was a term driven into us by John Hejduk, an influential educator. He said that the most important aspect for any work is for it to be authentic. The public doesn't really know that. We have to do something to educate them about being discerning. Why would anyone want to live in an 18th century French country house and not live in the moment, the present that is representative of this time and place?

RON WOMMACK Martin Heidegger's papers talk about how technology is not this passive thing, but an aggressive utilitarian thing that's pursuing us all the time. The only way we as humans are going to survive that is appealing to our poetic, authentic side. What is it in what we do that makes us more human when we realize what we are? What makes us unique in that way? Then we can deal with all the other stuff that tries to dehumanize us like all the advertising and technology and all that. We are totally a visual society. What makes you more human than anything else is when all your senses are engaged. That's why people always say, "Gee, I love going to the mountains," because all your senses are going. It's not just about how everything looks, it's about how everything's operating at full capacity. That's when you feel human, or the most human, when all those things are working.

SHARON ODUM My goal, it seems in most of my projects, is to make them more accessible not just to my clients, but to the public. Hopefully it touches them in some way. Whether it's the way the light comes in or what the materials are or how they are put together, in some honest way. If these things that we make can be friendly and not a cold, brutal Modern which is the old Modern, I think we have a better chance of reaching more people.

EDWARD M. BAUM I believe that architects historically, not just today, but almost always have gotten their ideas across not by organizing and not by mobilizing politicians, but by example, making certain buildings that are then either admired or thought to be profitable or good, and that are adopted widely. What Diane has done—and to a lesser extent maybe with individual projects the people around the table—has shown an alternative and presented it visibly in the marketplace, which is the old American way. What can we do? In a curious way I think the first and foremost is keep doing what we are doing, and that is making nice things, good things, if not affordable at least approachable by ordinary people. People can have a vision of themselves living here, giving people a model or an idea. Every time that happens the market gets a little bigger and the understanding gets there and expects you to question the ordinary stuff. It's very important that there is a culture of architecture and values. People respond if they see it.

# FACULTY

2002–2003

**Donald Gatzke**
Dean, Faculty of Architecture

**David Jones**
Associate Dean, Faculty of Architecture

**Jane Arhens**
Assistant Professor of Architecture

**Richard Atchison**
Lecturer in Architecture

**Ogden L. Bass**
Lecturer in Landscape Architecture

**Edward M. Baum**
Professor of Architecture

**Rebecca L. Boles**
Senior Lecturer in Interior Design

**Bill Boswell**
Associate Professor of Architecture

**Karen Bullis**
Assistant Professor of Architecture

**Roger Connah**
Visiting Assistant Professor of Architecture

**Anthony Cricchio**
Lecturer in Architecture

**Francois De Kock**
Visiting Assistant Professor in Landscape Architecture

**Mark R. Domiteaux**
Lecturer in Architecture

**Chester Duncan, Jr.**
Professor of Architecture

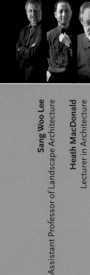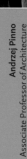

**Sang Woo Lee**
Assistant Professor of Landscape Architecture

**Heath MacDonald**
Lecturer in Architecture

**Micheal Malone**
Lecturer in Architecture

**Paul Manno**
Lecturer in Interior Design

**Jessie Marshall**
Lecturer in Architecture

**John P. Maruszczak**
Associate Professor of Architecture

**Gwen Mason**
Lecturer in Interior Design

**Mark McCollom**
Lecturer in Architecture

**John McDermott**
Professor of Architecture

**Medan Mehta**
Professor of Architecture

**Marian Millican**
Associate Professor of Interior Design
Director, Interior Design

**Cliford P. Mycoskie**
Lecturer in Landscape Architecture

**Andrew Nance**
Lecturer in Architecture

**Andrzej Pinno**
Associate Professor of Architecture

John Fain
Lecturer in Landscape Architecture

John M. Ferguson
Lecturer in Architecture

R.B. Ferrier
Professor of Architecture

Elfriede Foster
Instructor in Interior Design

Jess R. Galloway
Visiting Professor in Architecture

George Gintole
Associate Professor of Architecture

Raymond Joe Guy
Associate Professor of Architecture

R. Todd Hamilton
Professor of Architecture

Jay Henry
Professor of Architecture

C. Hill
Lecturer in Architecture

George T. James
Senior Lecturer in Architecture

Jim Johnson
Lecturer in Architecture

Craig Kuhner
Professor of Architecture

Jerald Kunkel
Senior Lecturer in Architecture

Martha LaCess
Professor of Architecture

Steve Lawson
Senior Lecturer in Architecture

Martin Price
Professor of Architecture

Steve Quevedo
Assistant Professor of Architecture

Ronald Reynolds
Adjunct Assistant Professor in Landscape Architecture

Mark Roberson
Lecturer in Architecture

Gary Robinette
Associate Professor of Landscape Architecture

Thomas V. Rusher
Lecturer in Architecture

Mohammad A. Salam
Lecturer in Landscape Architecture

Jeffery Sudman
Lecturer in Architecture

Pat Taylor
Associate Professor of Landscape Architecture
Director, Landscape Architecture

Barbara von der Heydt
Lecturer in Architecture

Jeff Whatley
Lecturer
Technical Staff Assistant

C. Lee Wright, Jr.
Associate Professor of Architecture
Director, Architecture

Michael Yardley
Associate Professor of Architecture

Bijan Youssefzadeh
Visiting Professor

# Bachelor of Science in Architecture     >

Hurst, Texas

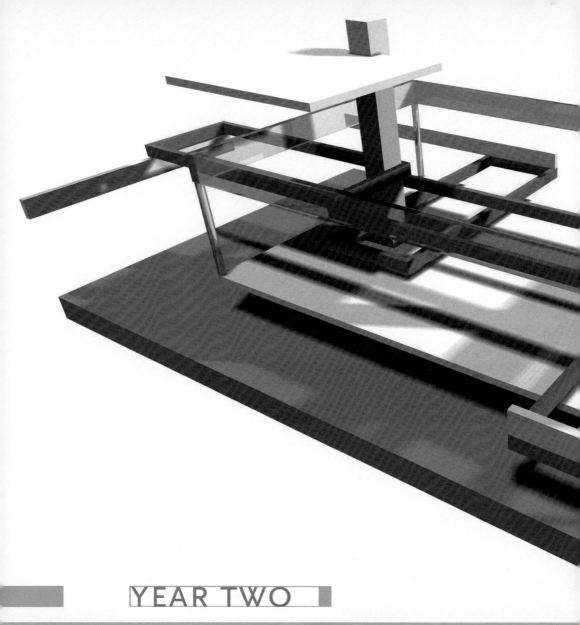

# YEAR TWO

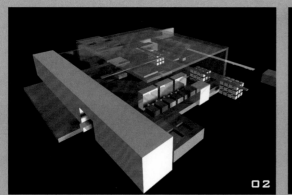

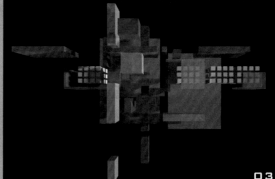

Architectural Design and Drawing I and II introduce students to design, design drawing, and color theory utilizing lectures and studio exercises. The two semester sequence examines the intersection between abstract formal principles and process methodologies. In the first semester two- and three-dimensional studio exercises develop a sensibility to design fundamentals and vocabulary, leading to the small-scale spatial and architectural applications of the second semester.

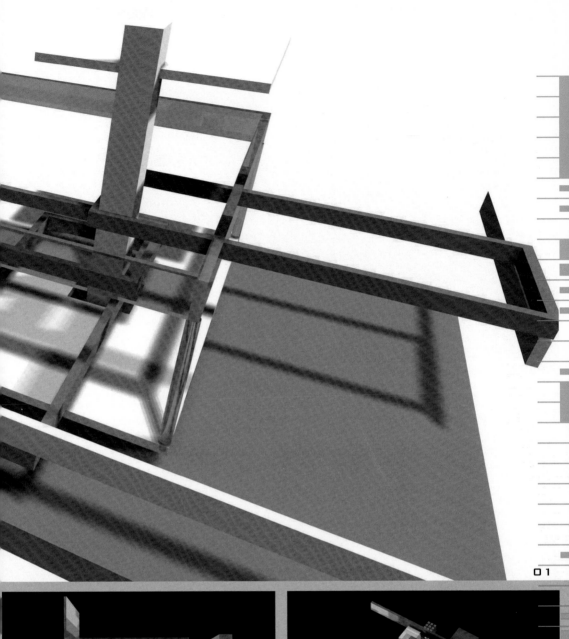

01

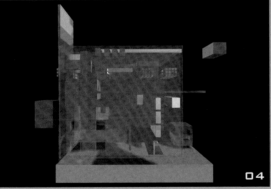

04

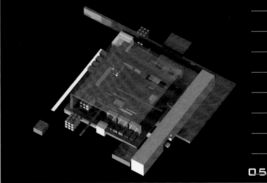

05

## [studio.architecture]
**DESIGN AND DRAW** I
CRITIC. Thomas Rusher

STUDENTS. 01. Johnson Nakia,
02–04. Sammy Langkop

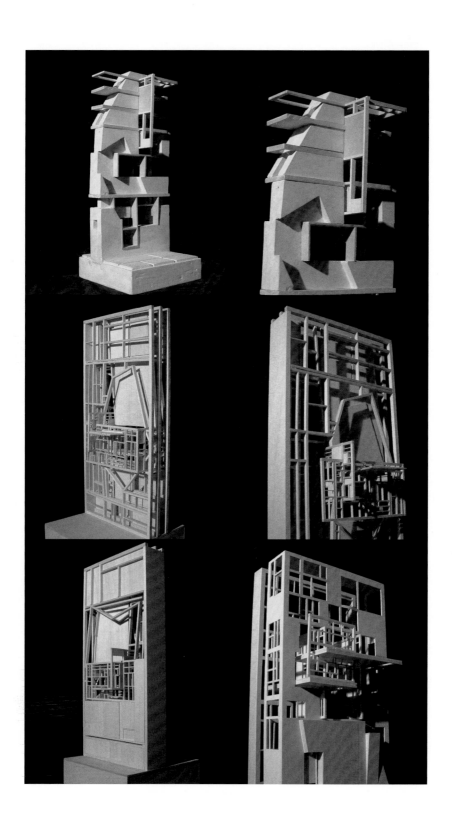

# [**studio**.architecture]
**DESIGN AND DRAW I**
CRITIC. Andrew Nance
Spring 2003

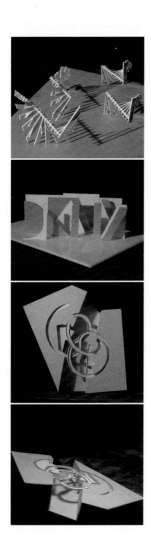

# [**studio**.architecture]
**DESIGN AND DRAW II**
CRITIC. Martin Price
Spring 2002

STUDENTS. Zindy Infante, Migena Dilolli, Adam Hillman

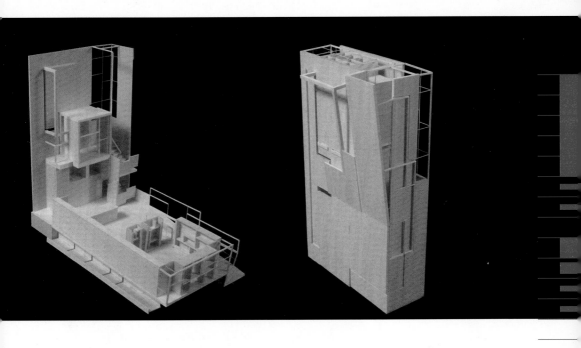

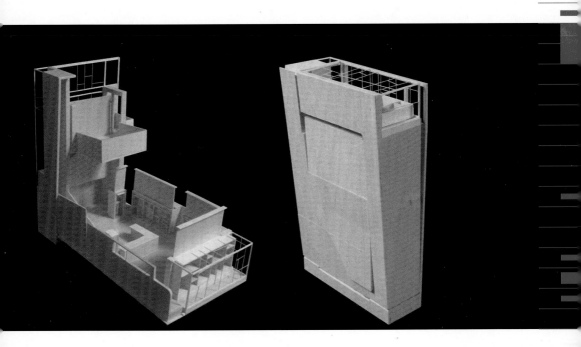

# [**studio**.architecture]
**DESIGN AND DRAW I**
CRITIC. Heath MacDonald
Fall 2003

STUDENTS. Paul Baca, Michael Kosbab

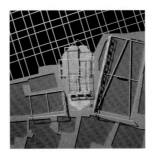

# YEAR THREE

Design Studios Architecture I and II enable an in depth investigation and application of basic design principles and spatial concepts toward the synthesis of simple building types. With an increased complexity and scale of projects, the second semester of the third year incorporates a variety of design theory, site conditions and technical considerations.

**[studio.**architecture**]**
**DESIGN STUDIO II**
CRITIC. Andrew Nance
Spring 2002

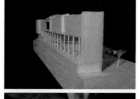

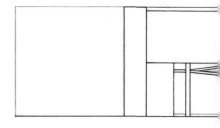

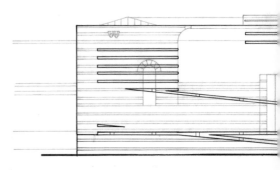

# [**studio**.architecture]
**DESIGN STUDIO I**
CRITIC. Steve Quevedo
Spring 2003

STUDENTS. Taisuke Tsuji, Richard Jones

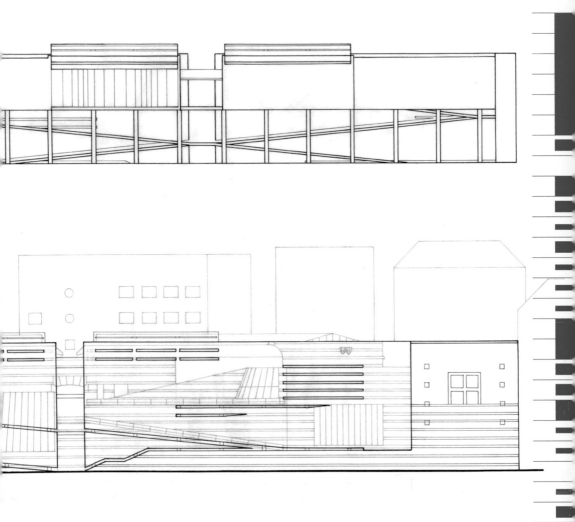

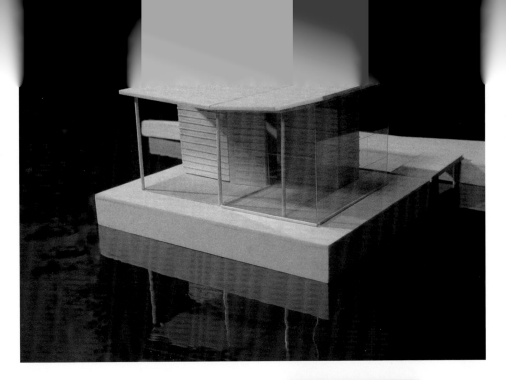

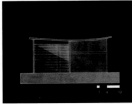

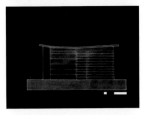

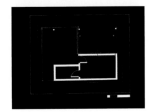

# [**studio**.architecture]
**DESIGN STUDIO I**
CRITIC. Anthony Cricchio
Fall 2003

STUDENTS. Aubrey Hartman, Jeffery Pardue, Marcy
Sandberg, Christopher Sias

Miguel Perez
Second Place Bienal Miami + Beach
*International design Boathouse
Competition 2003*

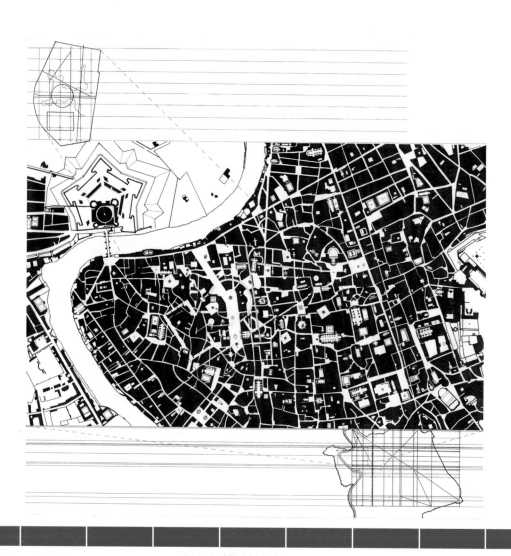

# [studio.architecture]
### DESIGN STUDIO II
CRITIC. Steve Quevedo
Fall 2003

STUDENTS. Asuka Aratake, Jared Brown, Nicholas Cate, Sarah Frank, Ruben Garcia, Kenny Martin, Marcus McKenzie, Sergio Molina, Douglas Payne, Alfredo Peña, James Perry, Teresa Ritter, Rogelio Sotelo

# [**studio**.architecture]
**DESIGN STUDIO I**
CRITIC. David Jones
Spring 2003

STUDENTS. James Perry, Marcus McKenzie

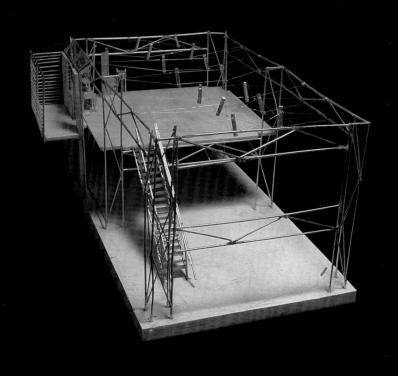

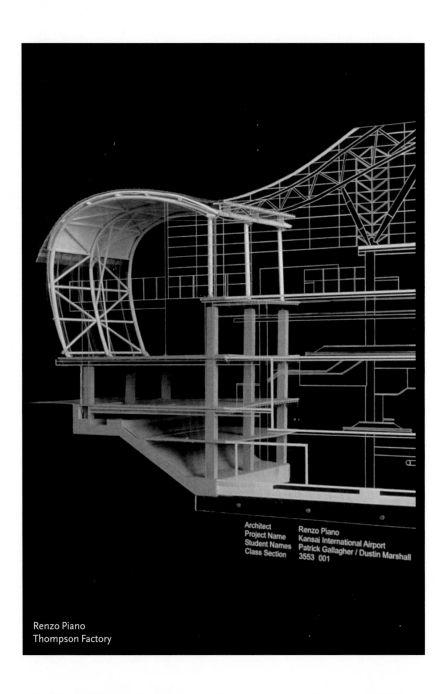

Architect        Renzo Piano
Project Name     Kansai International Airport
Student Names    Patrick Gallagher / Dustin Marshall
Class Section     3553  001

Renzo Piano
Thompson Factory

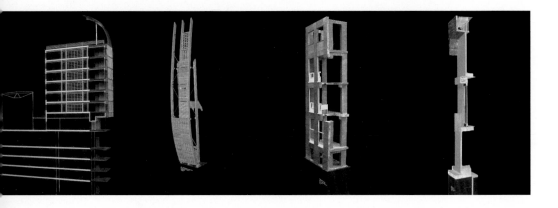

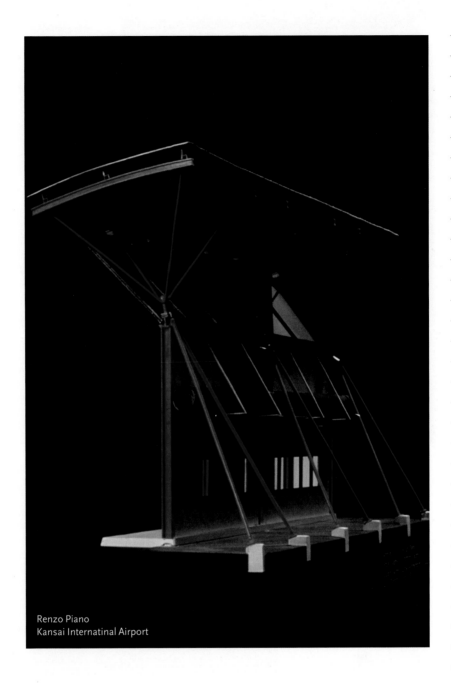

Renzo Piano
Kansai Internatinal Airport

# [studio.architecture]

**DESIGN STUDIO I**
*Case Study Section Models*
CRITICS. Heath MacDonald, Steve Quevedo
Spring 2003

STUDENTS. Lena Gershengoren, Rudy Lopez,
Patrick Gallagher, Dustin Marshall

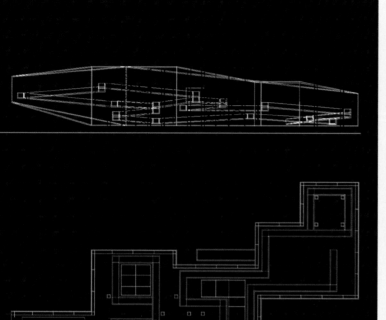

# [**studio**.architecture]
**DESIGN STUDIO I**
CRITIC. Karen Bullis
Fall 2002

STUDENT. Ronnie Parsons

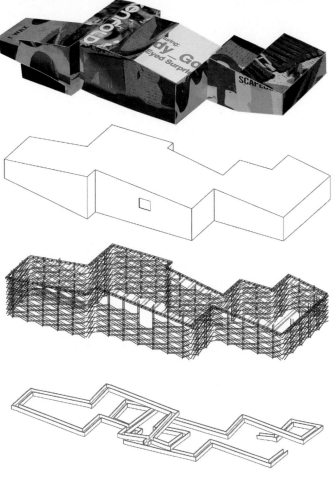

01

02

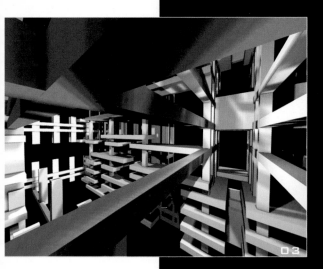

03

04

05

[digital.design]
DESIGN COMMUNICATION II
CRITIC. Thomas Rusher
Fall 2003

STUDENTS. 01 Dian Sutedjo
02 Jared Jones
03 Adele Cuartelon
04 Jared Jones
05 Ryan Curtis
06 Kenta Aoki
07 Jared Jones

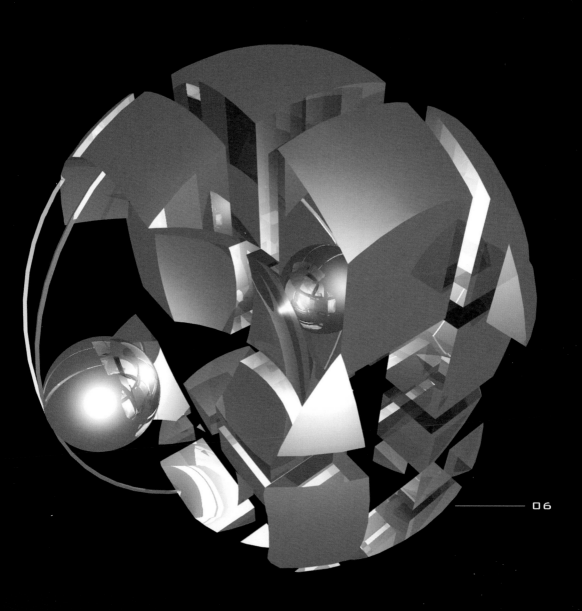

——————— 06

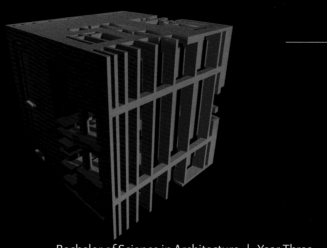

——————— 07

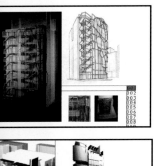

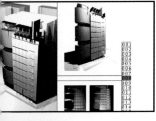

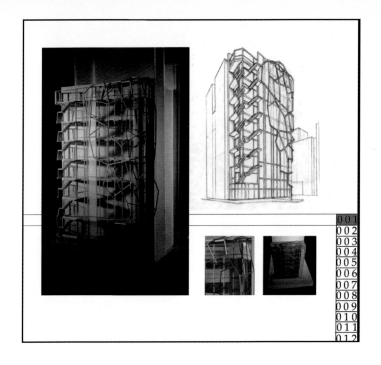

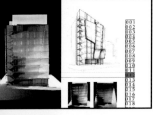

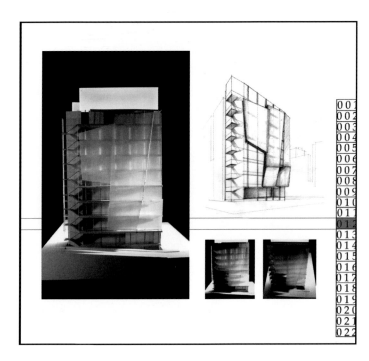

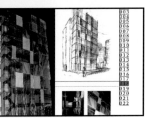

# YEAR FOUR

Design Studios Architecture III and IV offer the first opportunity for students to select both a studio project and instructor outside of a fixed sequence. The fourth year advanced architectural design problems range in scale, design strategy and approach. Projects examine programming schematic organization, synthesis and design of buildings in their environmental context.

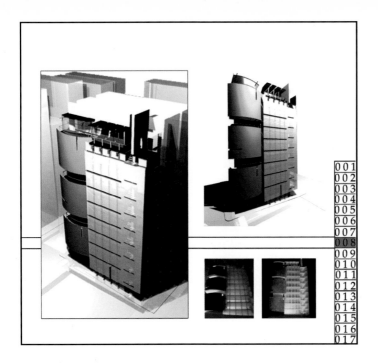

001
002
003
004
005
006
007
008
009
010
011
012
013
014
015
016
017

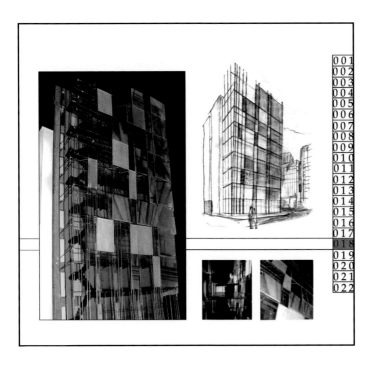

001
002
003
004
005
006
007
008
009
010
011
012
013
014
015
016
017
018
019
020
021
022

# [**studio**.architecture]
**DESIGN STUDIO IV**
CRITIC. Richard Ferrier
Spring 2003

STUDENTS. Heather Perry, Jazheel Fuentes, Jose Luis Padilla, David Muñoz, Josua J. Prosperie

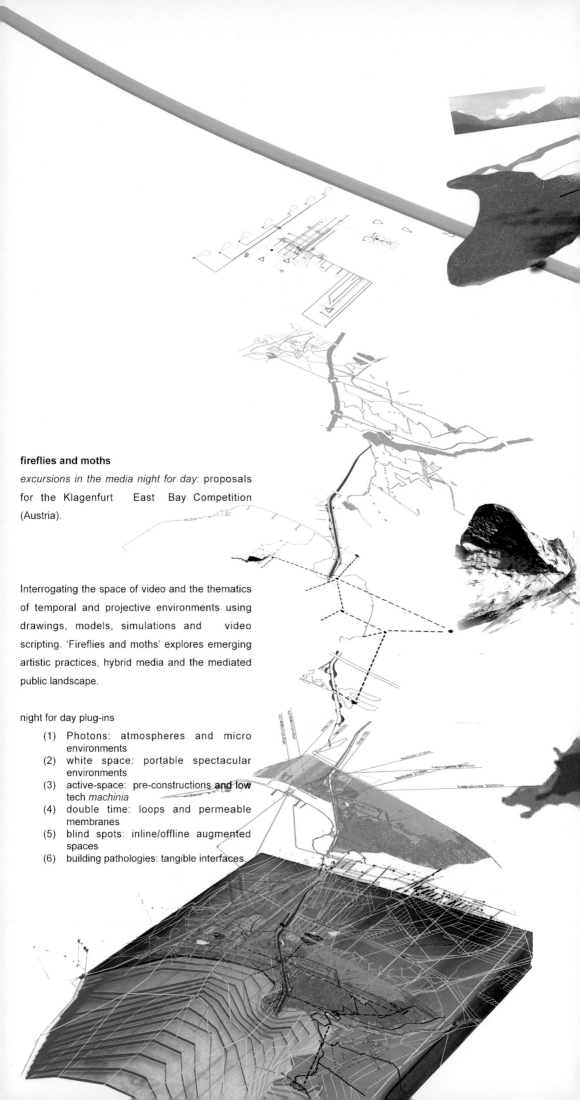

**fireflies and moths**

*excursions in the media night for day:* proposals for the Klagenfurt East Bay Competition (Austria).

Interrogating the space of video and the thematics of temporal and projective environments using drawings, models, simulations and video scripting. 'Fireflies and moths' explores emerging artistic practices, hybrid media and the mediated public landscape.

night for day plug-ins

- (1) Photons: atmospheres and micro environments
- (2) white space: portable spectacular environments
- (3) active-space: pre-constructions **and low** tech *machinia*
- (4) double time: loops and permeable membranes
- (5) blind spots: inline/offline augmented spaces
- (6) building pathologies: tangible interfaces.

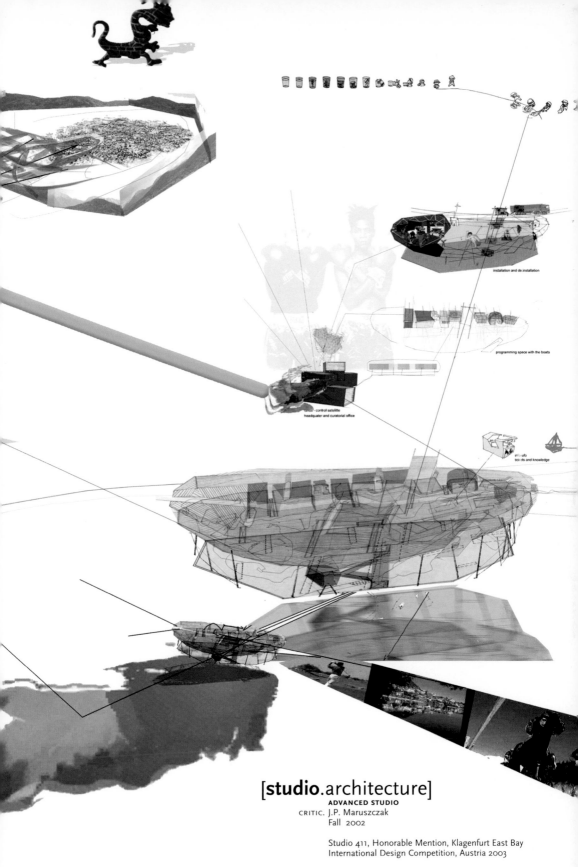

# [studio.architecture]
### ADVANCED STUDIO
CRITIC. J.P. Maruszczak
Fall 2002

Studio 411, Honorable Mention, Klagenfurt East Bay
International Design Competition, Austria 2003

STUDENT. Simon Oberhammer

**lab-o-matics**

*labs, habs & pre-f(labs)*

Amphibious Miami-    *proposals for the* Miami
Beach Bienal 2003

an investigation of floating, controlled chance-
dynamics of reactive  amphibious  structures and
the conditions of weightlessness .

a double laboratory: a test site of the 'way things
go' and a mirror-networked web of interactive
collaborations, experimental methodologies and
augmented spatial  proposals.

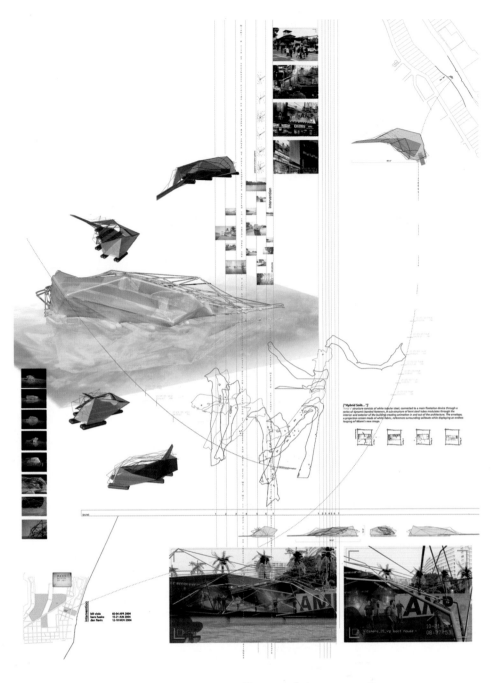

# [studio.architecture]
## ADVANCED STUDIO
CRITIC. J.P. Maruszczak
Fall 2003

STUDENTS. Rey Castillo + Jared White
Honorable Mention Bienal Miami+Beach
International Design Competition 2003

Rachel Antebi + Michael Garrett
Honorable Mention Bienal Miami+Beach
International Design Competition 2003

Isaco Perez Sosa
Honorable Mention Bienal Miami+Beach
International Design Competition 2003

Ronnie Parsons + Martin Skalet
Tania Rodallegas + Jesse Rodriguez
Yu-ming Mao + Abby Richardson

**thehotelarchitecture.com** is a studio-in-progress - the words 'hotel' and 'architecture' are used in their widest, most inventive, even dangerous meanings. lectures, film screenings, readings, mappings - we navigate through ignorance as much as awareness, stupidity as much as sovereignty, arrival as much as departure. there is always an enigma to any departure, an anxiety about arrival and a thrill at travelling as different understandings of how (a work of) architecture in its widest sense begins and concludes. The works attempt to defer that arrival whilst occupying conditions we call architecture. each student is involved in a 'work in progress' for their imaginary hotel architecture - if the result is postponed, incomplete, random, of partial or no destination, can that process itself be architecture? and where might the current poetics of movement, unrest, discontinuity or displacement fit in such architectural undressing? each idea, notion for the hotel is attacked and assaulted as if it is an 'architecture' that has arrived before another architecture sets in - for example hotel anxiety, hotel temperament, hotel silence, hotel transit, hotel paternoster, hotel interactive, hotel fame, hotel event, hotel information, hotel chance - each word becomes a work-in-progress, a word-world which dissembles, openly explodes, interrogates and then takes to its extreme the conventional notions of architecture and the hotel - later these notions re-converge toward a re-assembly of known and unknown architectural solutions - the aim here is not only to understand how a hotel functions but how its metaphor may be used as a model for a perpetually, re-programmed, re-invented architectural task and response.

# [**studio**.architecture]
**ADVANCED STUDIO**
CRITIC. Roger Connah
Spring 2001

hotel temperament project: John Humpreys

organization

foundations
(exist)

foundations
(altered)

density
(exist)

density (altered)

density (new)

Existing

Ne

"Obeli-terns"

Eat waste.

Build waste.

"It's not a parking lot..."

Work waste.

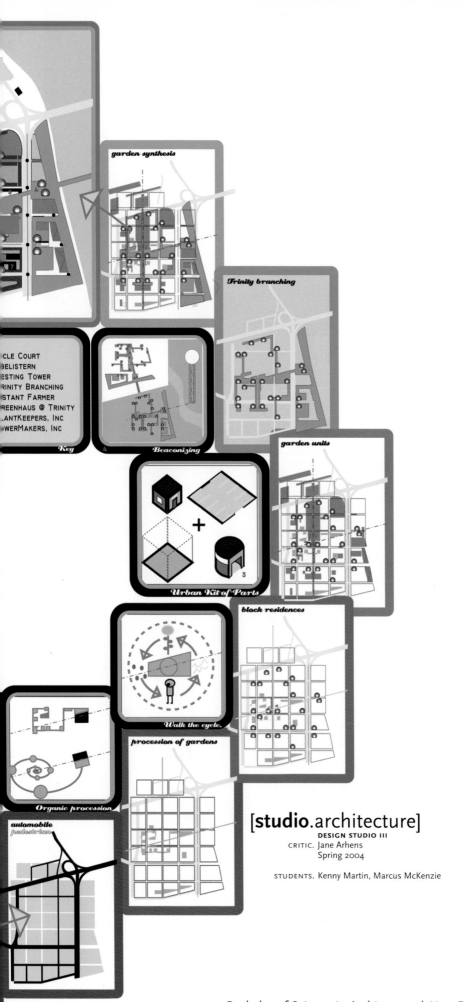

garden synthesis

Trinity branching

CLE COURT
BELISTERN
ESTING TOWER
RINITY BRANCHING
STANT FARMER
REENHAUS @ TRINITY
ANTKEEPERS, INC
WERMAKERS, INC

Key

Beaconizing

garden units

Urban Kit-of-Parts

block residences

Walk the cycle.

Organic procession

procession of gardens

automobile
pedestrian

**[studio.**architecture**]**
**DESIGN STUDIO III**
CRITIC. Jane Arhens
Spring 2004

STUDENTS. Kenny Martin, Marcus McKenzie

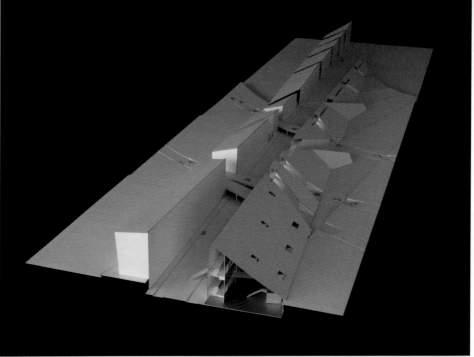

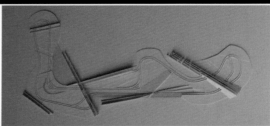

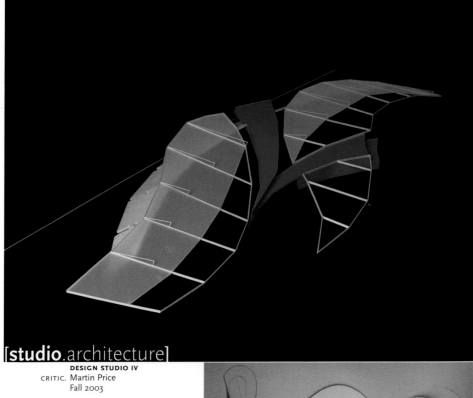

# [studio.architecture]
**DESIGN STUDIO IV**
CRITIC. Martin Price
Fall 2003

STUDENTS. Jan Damiecki, Jason Arndt

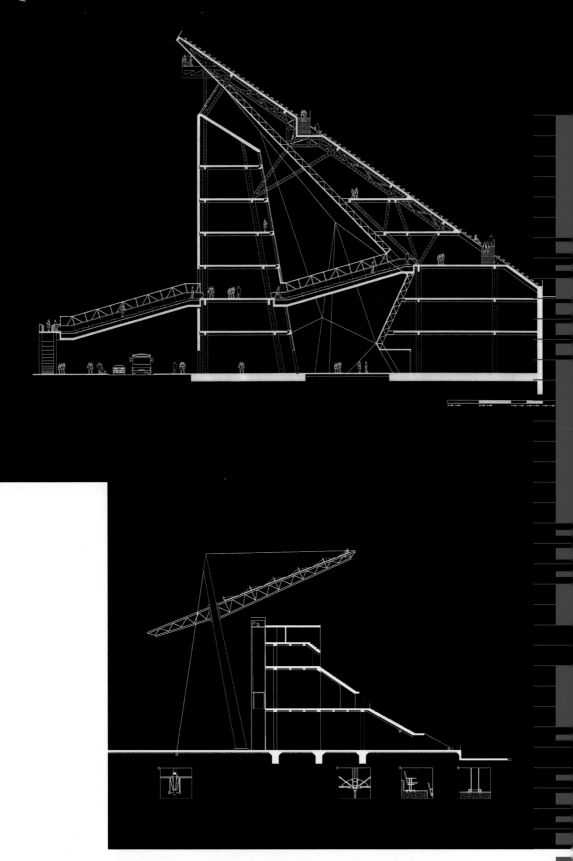

WEAVING INTO THE MEANDERING MOVEMENT OF A GRAND PRIX ROAD
RACE TRACK FOR WAXAHACHIE.

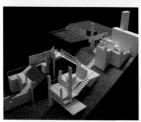

# [**studio**.architecture]
**DESIGN STUDIO IV**
CRITIC. R. Todd Hamilton
Fall 2003

STUDENTS. Randall Daniel, Jay Orelup, Jared White

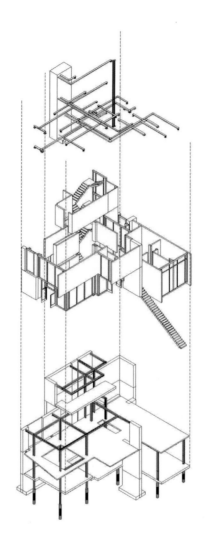

# [**studio**.architecture]
**DESIGN STUDIO III**
CRITIC. Bill Boswell
Fall 2002

STUDENTS. Alejandro Call, Casey Carlton, Julie Seamer,
Mario Guerrero

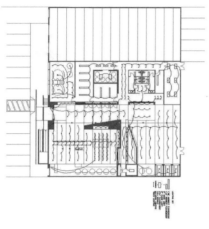 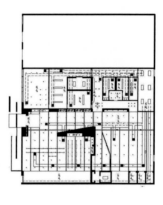

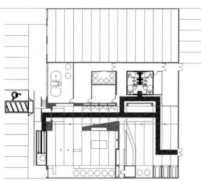 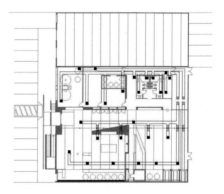

# [**studio**.architecture]
**DESIGN STUDIO III**
CRITIC. Bill Boswell
Fall 2002

STUDENTS. Alejandro Call, Casey Carlton, Julie Seamer,
Mario Guerrero

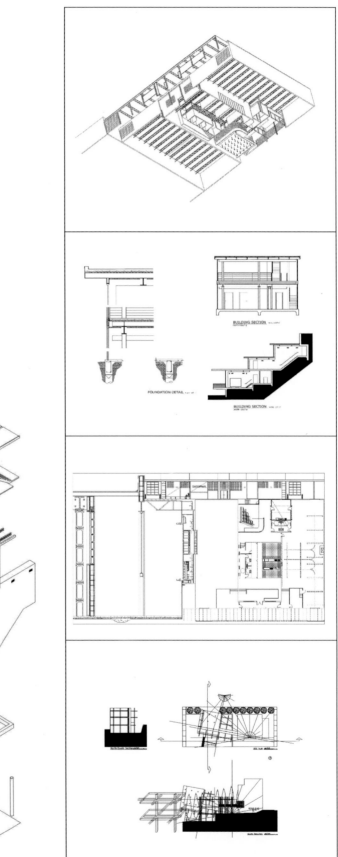

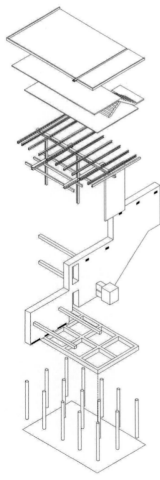

**Metro Constellations**

*proposals for the 13<sup>th</sup>* Takiron International Design
Competition, Temporary Permanent House

exploring short–life space  as a transformative
urban scenario and a provisional architecture of
the home.

Stress sites: video polytychs and online games as
a crash culture primer of  dust, noise and manic
lifestyles.

Strange Weather: improvisational maps of
unknown quantities, disaster in the metroplexed
urban environment of erasure and digitization

Home Alone Redux: inter-performance scores of
durational  structures and hacker  ready-mades as
a cartography of (un)inhabitable places.

shelf-life short li

# [**studio**.architecture]
### ADVANCED STUDIO
CRITIC. J.P. Maruszczak
Fall 2001

STUDENTS. Bryan Wren, Honorable Mention, Temporary
Permanent House, Takiron International Design
Competition, 2002

Tobias Magnesco, Angelika Mair, Andreas
Moling, Melanie Pratt, Melody Yiu

sell-by life short fuse

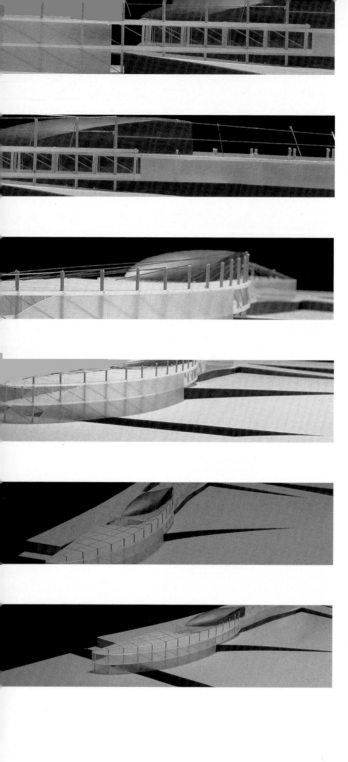

# [**studio**.architecture]
**DESIGN STUDIO IV**
CRITIC. George Gintole
Fall 2003

STUDENT. Jose Tejeda

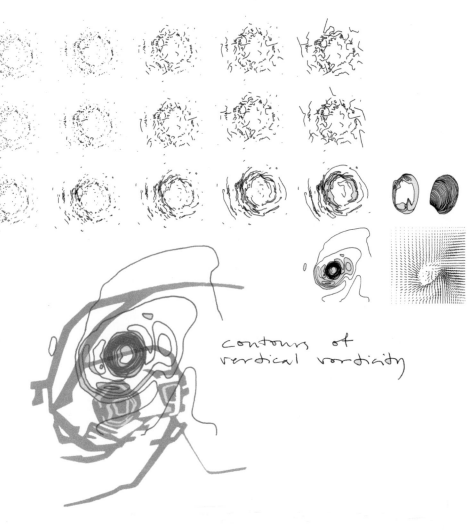

contours of
vertical vorticity

Tri State Tornado
march 18, 1925
1pm – 5pm

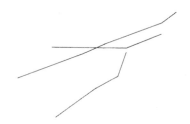
garden of destruction

Fort Worth Tornado
march 28, 2000

Moore Tornado
may 3, 1999
4.45 first tornado → 6 hours
at least one tornado
would be on the ground
at every moment
except for one two min lull.

garden of construction

The following is a selection from the March 2, 2004, UT Arlington symposium "Architectural Concrete" with FRED LANGFORD, consultant to Louis I. Kahn on the Salk Institute in La Jolla, California, the Kimbell Art Museum in Fort Worth and the Capital complex at Dacca; TOM SEYMOUR, past president of Thos. S. Byrne, Inc., responsible for the construction of the Kimbell Art Museum from 1969–72; and PAUL SIPES, Vice President of Linbeck and Senior Project Manager for the construction of the Modern Art Museum of Fort Worth. The symposium was organized and moderated by W. MARK GUNDERSON, AIA, an architect in Fort Worth.

# Dialogue two

## Architectural Concrete
### *The Pursuit of Perfection*

**W. MARK GUNDERSON** At the outset we can say, "What if the issue of architectural concrete's perfection had to do with only the face finish of the concrete?" I say "what if" because we have had conversations here using the Salk Institute as a perfect example. The addition to the Salk done by Anshen and Allen achieved an almost mirror smooth polished face. You have to ask if that's any better than the original building. To what extent is a perfectly smooth finish relevant? In fact, Tadao Ando's concerns at the Modern are telling in that regard.

**PAUL SIPES** His concern was with the ultimate finish. In everything we saw that he has done in Japan the goal was to have a smooth finish. There was also the concern to compliment the Kimbell and so that medium was selected at the beginning.

**W. MARK GUNDERSON** But his buildings in Japan don't have, necessarily, that kind of finish. The joint work between the forms is not so perfectly aligned.

**PAUL SIPES** The joining of panel to panel in Japan is, I would say, fairly casual as compared to the Kimbell or what we did at the Modern. When you discuss that with them they say generally, "That's our older work, that's the previous work. Our work is evolving and we're looking to achieve the flat, very smooth line from pour to pour and from panel to panel."

**FRED LANGFORD** I had the privilege of seeing the Modern for the first time today and it's a beautiful building and beautiful, exquisite concrete work. In contrast to, say, Lou Kahn's philosophy, there are certain huge monolithic pours that were extremely difficult I'm sure for Paul where you take a wall 24 to 30-foot-high and put the portals in it and block-outs and get everything lined up. It took a lot of walers and strong backs to hold that in place to accept all this concrete. It was well done. I think Kahn would have looked at it and said, "Maybe we can take it in certain pieces and come up to the top of a portal, stop there and go again." That next pour becomes a lintel over the door and so forth expressing the sequence of construction in a simpler way. I got the feeling in the Modern, that Ando would have one wish and that would be to form the whole complete building, dump in all the concrete, and then take the forms down and throw them away.

**PAUL SIPES** Absolutely.

**FRED LANGFORD** There wasn't an effort to take the pieces in increments to put it together.

**PAUL SIPES** They did not want to be able to read how the walls and the ceilings were divided to be able to build them. That was supposed to be seamless and invisible and for the most part I believe it is. Lots of time was spent discussing where we wanted to make a construction joint and obviously our first focus was ease of formwork, being able to reinforce it, and what the impact from one pour to the other might have on the elevation of the continuous wall.

**W. MARK GUNDERSON** In Lou's work I think the joint was the very first thing. The concrete vault span at the Kimbell, at one hundred feet, is about as far as you can go without introducing a control joint. For Kahn the materials determine the dimensions of the building. The joint very much drives the thing.

**PAUL SIPES** The only joint [at the Modern] indicated on the contract documents, the design documents, is the horizontal joint at the second floor line that is 18 feet in the air. All the vertical joints were created during the construction process but that horizontal joint was the only one that's indicated on the documents.

**TOM SEYMOUR** Mr. Kahn liked his buildings to define or at least show the way they were built. In other words, if there's going to be a joint he wanted it to be a joint—not try to hide it. We elected to use standard ¾-inch plyform and then we veneered the inside surface of that with ⅜-inch Marine plywood. Marine plywood is different from regular plywood in that it doesn't have any knot holes in it. We then beveled it where the joints would normally be to fit the pattern that he wanted. The only way we could convince him to do this was if we would then, when we were through casting, take that Marine plywood, ⅜-inch, and nail it as the decking on top of the cycloid shells. That would be the sub-deck under the lead sheathing. He bought into this so we used those liners ultimately permanently in the building rather than discarding them like you normally would. To achieve the slick surface he wanted, we experimented and we ended up using a polyurethane-type coating that we applied in our casting yard. When we got through with it all and we looked at it, you could see from start to finish and one end of the member to the other where the work was done. We didn't try to hide those joints. The building moves so you need to have a defined joint that can take the expansion and contraction that you're going to get. In this area there's a nearly 200-degree differential in temperature. In the winter it gets down maybe below zero and in the summer it's 100-degrees outside but if you get up on that roof it's like 160-degrees. There's a big difference and so concrete will move. It has to be designed to take that into account.

**W. MARK GUNDERSON** If I'm not mistaken, you actually have two different qualities of plywood. You

them to Komendant's office to check. There was a question about how many strands were in this tendon. In the conversation he says, "I want seven." So the guy wrote in seven, submitted it, and it came back approved. All these tendons were made up with seven strands. They were set in place, all ready to pour. Then we had a labor dispute and we had to not work for a couple of days. Fortunately Mr. Kahn was coming to town and he asked Komendant to come with him. We picked him up at the hotel and brought him out at the job. As we go along the job down to the superintendent's office to get the hardhats he said, "I want to see this pour." It was the south end, the gallery floor. So I get out of the car and he looks at it and he says, "My god! It's all wrong, it's all wrong!" We got him to calm down and he spotted the fact that there were only seven strands in these tendons that were supposed to have eleven. Everybody was pointing fingers at everybody as to why it happened. When all the smoke cleared away, it was just a simple misunderstanding of his answer, "Well, how many strands, Dr. Komendant?" "I want *eleven*." The guy thought he said seven and that's what he wrote down. The good Lord was looking out after us because I don't know what would have happened. Nobody would have known probably that we were shy four strands and then if we'd poured the concrete it would've been covered up.

**W. MARK GUNDERSON** And it just happened.

**TOM SEYMOUR** But he was a very sharp-eyed guy. And I'll tell you one thing about Mr. Kahn, he did not give Dr. Komendant the credit he deserved. There were some ill feelings over that. He was a Ph.D. doctor and he was one of Patton's engineers. When Patton was chasing the Germans back up over the mountains and blowing up the bridges behind him, well, Dr. Komendant would go along with the engineers and calculate the beam sizes on the bridges so that the U.S. engineers could rebuild them. The fact that he was just able to saunter up, look out there and see, those tendons are wrong. We were so lucky that he spotted that.

**FRED LANGFORD** How did you fix it?

**TOM SEYMOUR** We tore them out. We took them all out, ordered the right ones and went down and worked on the other side. The whole order was wrong.

**W. MARK GUNDERSON** But you happened to have an extra week.

**TOM SEYMOUR** We took it, we didn't like it but we had to take all those strands out and the tendon people were very good. They worked around the clock and got them up there in a couple of days. Fortunately they had the material to do it.

**PAUL SIPES** Most cable today is seven strands by the way.

**FRED LANGFORD** When Komendant would come to the office you'd hear him all over. His voice was booming and Lou would be suggesting something and you'd hear, "No, it'll go broke!" I guess you heard him say that. He was a character.

■

# Bachelor of Science in Interior Design $\quad$ >

Modern Art Museum of Fort Worth, Texas

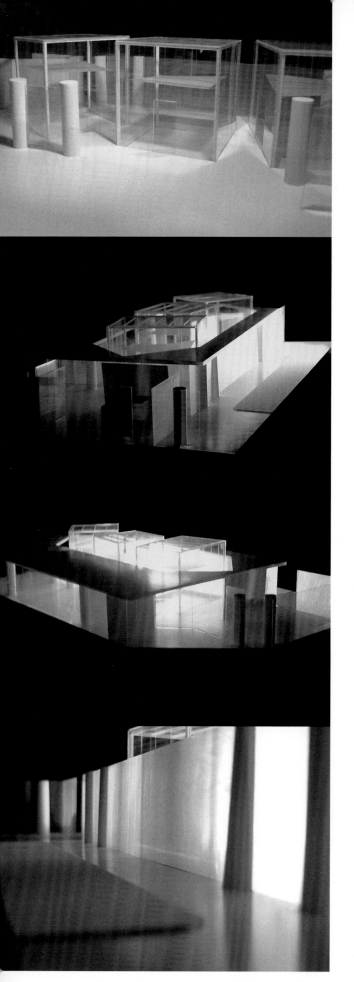

## [studio.interiors]
**DESIGN STUDIO III**
CRITIC. Elfriede Foster
Fall 2003

STUDENTS. Michele Blose, Paula Vair

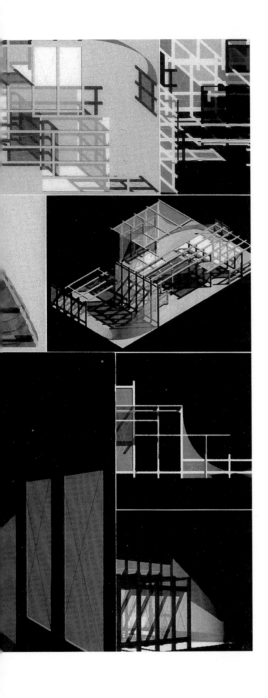

**[studio.**interiors]
**DESIGN STUDIO III**
CRITIC. Elfriede Foster
Fall 2003

STUDENT. Jean McClure

# [studio.interiors]
### FURNITURE STUDIO
CRITICS. Rebecca Boles, Jeff Whatley
Spring 2003

STUDENTS. Brent Anderson, Bonnie
Wampler, Lisette Alviar,
Clifton Crofford

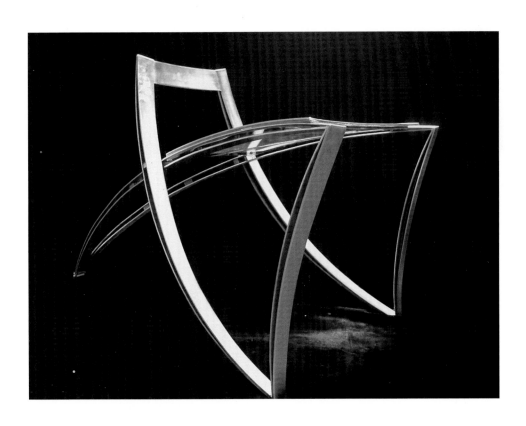

# [**studio**.interiors]
**INTERIOR DETAILING**
CRITIC. Rebecca Boles
Fall 2002

STUDENTS. David Hook, Bonnie Wampler

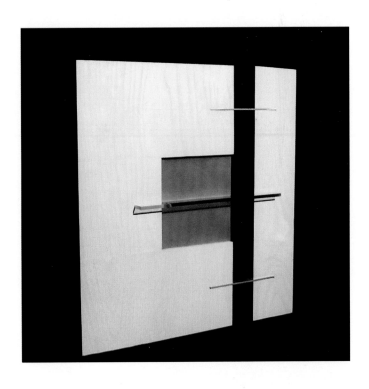

# Dialogue three

## Edwin Chan Speaks to Students

**MARTIN PRICE** We had a nice discussion today. We visited the Nasher Sculpture Garden and then we went to the Modern, and the Kimbell.

**EDWIN CHAN** I made him do all that with me.

**MARTIN PRICE** It wasn't very difficult taking someone like Edwin. We had some discussions about conditions at these places—about what makes a building or an environment comfortable and not comfortable? How do you place sculpture in a garden?

**EDWIN CHAN** Yesterday I was in Houston and every time I go to Houston I go to the Menil Collection. I think that is Renzo Piano's masterpiece. I saw it for the first time, actually, with Frank [Gehry] in 1996. When you go to a museum with Frank you do the whole thing in 20 minutes. This time I arrived in Houston a day early so I actually could spend a little bit of time in the museum. For me that was a much better museum than the Nasher. I follow the Piano museums because he's a good architect. I want to learn other ways of doing museums other than the way we do them ... and he's a good role model. So we've also looked at the Beyeler Collection in Basel. It is a very similar kind of museum in the sense that he took the theme from Kahn, the parallel walls, and reinvented the natural lighting system. What makes the Menil Collection better than the other ones is it was the first one ... so he was still figuring it out and that gave it a sort of energy. It was much more of a sketch—and every time he repeats the theme it gets to be a little bit more refined and it gets to be a little bit more fussy. And that, for us, was distracting for the art. The other thing I like a lot about the Menil Collection was that the collection itself was very moving—the mixture—it's not just Modern art, it's got Surrealist stuff, it's got the African stuff, it's got the Classical stuff. The way the art is juxtaposed and displayed and its relationship with the light well that is whole space. They used to say it doesn't work for paintings because of inadequate viewing space.

**EDWIN CHAN** I saw it work beautifully for paintings. What they mean is it is a pain in the ass to hang paintings. Which is a different statement than it doesn't work. What they need to do is float the paintings in front of the wall. The problem with that is that it trivializes the whole conversation into a question of logistics.

**MARTIN PRICE** It's not a very large space. The photographs make it look larger than it is. In some ways it is rather intimate.

**EDWIN CHAN** Oh, totally intimate. Your point about the Frick is a very important one. It goes back to another conversation that we always get involved with, which is neutral space. If you think about museums and art and you look back in history the first museums were essentially big houses. The Frick, what we like about it, the scale of it is essentially the scale of a big house. One of the best museums is John Soane's house in London. Another beautiful museum is the Picasso Museum in Paris, a big French hotel. The Rodin Museum, in Paris, is another house with a beautiful sculpture garden. No one would argue with you when you say, "I love the Picassos in the Picasso Museum," or you like the Rodin in the Rodin Museum.

**MARTIN PRICE** So it's a fallacy that many architects have, that art needs to have a neutral background.

**EDWIN CHAN** I don't think the issue is whether the background is neutral or not. Everyone would agree the museum, the gallery, or the place should complement the art, it should make the art come alive. A neutral background is not the only way to do it. In some cases you can do that. Most art looks better in a strong context. You have to remember that when the artist created this stuff, the creative process was in vision and experience and not in a white neutral space. So it is a bit of a mythology. Now, I am not going to argue against a white neutral space, but there are other ways to think about it. The more important issue is what needs to be created to make the work come alive, to capture the spirit of the work. Again, that doesn't have to look like the Guggenheim by any means, but I think that the essence of it is that you are moving through volumes with different kinds of light. Sometimes you have north light, sometimes you have south light. And the nonrepetitious aspect of it makes the experience much more interesting. It is kind of like if you were to go through a city, what makes a democratic city work is that you have variety, and for me that is an important value.

# Master of Architecture     >

Dallas, Texas

**(Minneapolis 26.1.2004)**

I am sitting in Starbucks a few hours before Pulp Architecture goes to Minnesota. I feel no urge to restrain the talk. The architecture all around is of occasional but predictable brilliance, a kind of dismal competence. Gehry's Weisman Museum is carefully applied architecture, turning an assemblage and chaos into the container. Up close it neither impresses nor invokes all those wonderful readings and, of course, mis-readings. It reminds me of all those buildings that have been spoken about in laudatory terms, in phrases that should mean something but often don't. The trade-fair, silver-foil scaffolding of its applied skin looks like a cosmetic taken further in the Guggenheim in Bilbao. Surprise should not come to us so easily, so seductively, the geographer showing me the museum said. I prefer the Georgian Square, he continued. I preferred neither. Both have their moments but in this new century surely we can come up with something better.

You see, downtown, the computer programmer told me in the morning, you'll see the ugliest building in the whole metroplex. Here too, St.Paul and Minneapolis is called a metroplex. I disliked the word with its hint at the metropolitan that was nowhere to be seen, or experienced. And which building was that? I asked. The ugliest? It mattered not, for the buildings, tall and small, all interchanged in the bleakness of the winter, the hard chill and the salted snow turning into blackened crust. In the film Deep Impact which I caught last night in the hotel, the tidal wave begins coming in after the comet has fallen. I imagined everyone in Minneapolis running along the skyways, running nowhere to escape the inevitable. Elsewhere, a long way from America a dear friend had shown a glimmer of hope in her otherwise lifelong struggle to avoid suicide. Her last two attempts had failed. The glimmer, that generous sign in the eyes, however small, is all she has. It is merely a trigger. But it can, it certainly can, be enough. Let's hope so.

Looking out from this café, from the softest armchair (the only one) I looked across at the atrium of the IDS centre. Surely architecture could not go on supporting such a willful loss of life, of time, even of disgust. The battle lines are drawn. We've had enough. It is only a matter of time before we take over. And beware. You've been warned. It will not be anything recognizable from the softest armchair in Starbucks.

# [beware:architecture]
Roger Connah

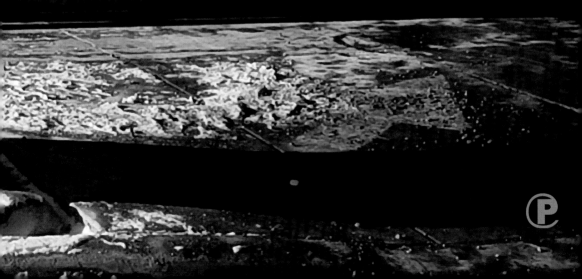

[**slash:**architecture]

9 why do we have to generate more and m

**15 why are we so comfortabl**

e image touches on memory, does architecture become part of the imagined event?
ould architecture require mastery of content and connection, links and loops?

8 why is the vis

the ecstasy of no further communication

# here

6 w                    of unrelated, growing data formed

22 why

# comes

26 why, if information

# the

# night

**night** is neither the eclipse we are so used to, nor the comfort of the body's rest. Just as we appear to be in a transitional phase, we suggest less the haste to define what is coming next, and prefer encounters with what might only be a partial destiny. And entering such destinies we try to understand how we operate – cognitively - within it. Locating this is a space of deferral where architecture is allowed the same conspiracy as night.

strative imagery? if data exists only t r a few seconds, should it be stored?

**etween, unfinished, restless and incomplete when we so obviously are not?**

**5 why is the constant development of connections import**

**29 why does architecture shaped from a digital impulse pretend to**

**uncontrolled, ncoherent and cacophony of forms**

various paths if you enjoy only one?

s are dynamically and digit

**[studio.**architecture**]**
ADVANCED DESIGN
CRITICS. J.P. Maruszczak, Roger Connah
Spring 2002

**night** of course must take on the very fear of architecture itself; the blindness of night. This is an imaginary encounter negotiated by navigating the poetics of night in Las Vegas, in the USA and in Europe, in Terezin, a town where night has almost remained in control of architecture itself.

# P. edagogics

Learning and higher learning have always attempted to relate theory to practice, but not always the other way round. Architecture has learnt the ability to apply itself; a kind of outreach of the expected and intuitive. Perhaps good theory is based on good practice, but what of the reverse? If practice itself is in flux, how does theory engage itself, how does research inform a closing world? Just where did the rift between education and practice begin; and does it help us identify the 'parti'? If we take on inter-disciplinarity, how can it be more than lip-service to the plural? If we remain en-shadowed in the privileged discourse and representation of known practice, is this closing the door on someone else's future? How can we learn to talk about the things that we love without cynicism, without the shelter of expected performance and known grievances? If we believe architecture can still build a better world, what is that better world we imagine? How can architecture reclaim its status, be altered and re-invented to meet new challenges without de-schooling architecture itself?

Do we need to control that better world to conform to our own imagination?

P.U.L.P offers a series of enquiries that explore the transition in architectural education and the changes in the profession. Using a laboratory method, the teaching atelier studio proposes research methodologies and self-assessment practices as a way for graduate students to come to terms with their own education and the future they cannot fully see but will certainly participate within, inside or outside the current profession of architecture. New structures, new building science, new, advanced technological solutions imply new access to information; it also implies a new savviness. How and where are students to learn this? What factors allow students to open to newness without being damned by novelty? Or seduced by the ease of applications? How does this meet the professional demands for education reform, and what then of the reverse? Is it hopeless to think education reform can alter professional operations? Surely the profession cannot be the only engine for change, evolution and renewal. Might not renewal demand a radical re-invention of architecture in its broadest terms, anticipated by some of the new contemporary, collaborative practices working around the world today? How and why do we wait until morphed architecture reaches the star circuit, to see it tickle down to studio and be born-again? How do we answer the profession's charge of the redundancy of students? And how does the profession answer the frustration of those who no longer want to enter the profession? Is the student derailed or the profession derailed? Or are there other futures, other networks where an architect renews engagement? Such studio methodology allows students to reflect on the framing of their own education, to direct their engagement and talents, and to make informed decisions about a career in a profession that changes the moment they graduate.

hctn + watp → u/s

## U. rgency

Urgency is an attractive interactive concept; it invites change which often takes much longer to implement. Our imaginations often run faster than the infrastructures that contain them. Frustration results, fatigue sets in as students navigate courses for credit to make the big escape. Architectural school is exile from mainstreet when mainstreet is already designed out of existence. Taking on the current ambiguity between a traditional design-based education, the desire for creative synthesis (aesthetic, social, ethical and technical) and the rise of new media techniques, the poetics and politics of architectural urgency are explored. Using and testing ideas across larger urban contexts (like Karachi and Nanjing) students learn to assess the new potential for planning, new mapping techniques, information and the tiredness of data, innovation processes, the relationships between landscapes and politics, advances in building and material science and new engineering structures. Issues such as sustainability, rehabilitation, trans-programming, disability, margins, activist groups and trans-urban strategies all contribute toward the complexities that make up contemporary practice. What then are the privileges implied in the use of such vocabulary? And how do language and vocabulary offer new operative strategies in contemporary practice? Or is this one more alienated  discourse? These do not necessarily replace previous methodologies but challenge precedent and complacency within both the education and the profession. The more immediate environments of Arlington, Fort Worth and Dallas are used as test-case communities and contexts for such thinking.

**[p.u.l.p.architecture]**
**ADVANCED DESIGN**
CRITICS. J.P. Maruszczak, Roger Connah
Spring 2002–04

## IS LARRY McMURTRY RIGHT?

*"When I left the Dallas-Fort Worth airport I slipped quickly through Arlington, not so much a city as an area of confusion that manages to combine the worst features of Dallas (just to the east) and Fort Worth (just to the west). My bitter dislike of Arlington goes back ten years, to a day when I embarrassed myself by getting hopelessly lost in it while attempting to take the world-famous, globally travelled author Jan Morris to lunch. Not long after this disgrace I complained about Arlington in a novel called Some Can Whistle, but nobody read that novel so no one heard my complaint. Passing through it again I noticed that it had become even uglier – my complaint, if anything, had been understated.*

intro    program    google

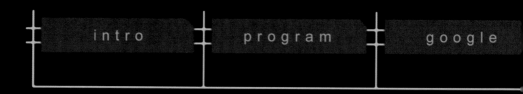

CALL OUT ARLINGTO.

X

there is a resistance, a fatigue to an architecture conventionalising, institutionalising too rapidly, there is a feeling that new architectures are only slipped in-between existing conventions

perhaps with all this flux going on
we have to be quick, quick to appropriate, to incorporate and to re-configure an unexpected architecture
or are we already too late? too cynical?

is trans-programming already an unnamed, uncomfortable reality? is the promise of the last century a model for the architecture of this? or can we operate like the hacker and alter the social and economic conditions cunningly?

under these circumstances, in a trans-urban zone called Arlington what might such architecture be? and – more importantly – what might it continue resisting to be? not an architecture that makes new urban conditions from old ones, not an architecture of the clever spectacle

perhaps an architecture of new events within which architecture re-situates itself within design and society, an architecture that re-programmes convention in Arlington, Texas, an architecture taking on partial destinies

as by-products become central, and ideas burn

# PULP ARCHITECTURE

**if for a moment!**

3          4          5          6

## L. iminal

That which is unformed is not necessarily ill-formed. The liminal is the space between one world and another; a space where one lingers like a sports arena, a cemetery or a hospital. It is commonly referred to as a transition zone. There has been so much talk of a new paradigm in the Thomas Kuhn sense of the word yet we still seem to be on the station waiting for it to arrive. But new paradigms no longer arrive in order that we safely step on. They creep upon us. They steal in the shadows of the comfortable applications we apply to known solutions and the seduction of those imaging tools which flatter the conventions celebrated. The very strategies and collaborative thinking coming out of this Liminal Zone in art, architecture, landscape, computer science and future studies, for example, suggest a new paradigm, even a new sensibility. This might then be the zone in which architecture has to dwell for years to come as it begins to negotiate its own existence as a profession. And all amidst reluctant collaborations with other disciplines! Thinking liminally allows us to explore new notions that respond to the transitional and provisional. This takes us on from the pragmatic notions of synthetic interventions and rehabilitation to more suggestive solutions; even to partial architectures and system architectures that demand increased response to global conditions, management scenarios, liberal arts failure. Architecture like Malraux's museum without walls, a work-in-progress, may no longer have any final form or completion; scattered, dispersed across a city already dispersed. The Liminal is also a parallel exercise into the way architecture can offer new responses to the liminal condition. Students explore how architecture might not only be the predetermined response to known briefs and unchanging environmental conditions but a strategy to take on wider, lateral thinking which equally demands from the student and the professor knowledge of the wider economic, investment, communicative and contractual conditions within which they, as part of collaborative teams in the future, may have to operate. Using the concept of liminality, challenging architecture on the edge, producing architecture from the edge, this explores a new contract in architectural practice which is informed from new building science, new structures, genetics, film, street (sub) cultures, art, play, the hacker ethic and new media. Respecting but rejecting the star architecture system of individualised, authored and over-revered spectacles, the range of this architecture is represented by diverse practices around the world today. And many more who wish to work in contemporary practice to think and feel their own way in the constant change they are presented with. That this architecture is indistinct, liminal, pulpy; that this has no 'official' or 'institutional' form, is no hindrance. Surely it is the gap within which the light gets through and the future re-scripts itself, rescued from cynicism and complacency.

## P. ortal

True they are seductive, they tilt and turn, flip and dive. The advertisers get there ahead of the architects and then the digital imaging software trickles back into an updated beaux-arts paradigm. Advances in visualization techniques, software and new media no longer only serve to promote or represent architecture of known quantity and quality in a more sophisticated, contemporary way. Thinking within these systems implies new thinking about data, information and the interactive space of architecture itself. This is not to be deceived by the easy opposition between the Virtual and the Real, an opposition almost constantly confused and blurred. The P.U.L.P. portal will set up a series of communicative devices, models, architectures and information systems that allow these ideas to be tested across other disciplines and within the architectural profession and education. Can we risk the failure of our own conceits? Can we accept that design is no longer the privilege of this profession, but the potential of greater networks? Is this an affront to the longstanding status of architecture as we know it? The Pulp Portal allows a glimpse of this self-questioning and a sneak preview of the potential of such systems defined by those working in the very media that makes the 'portal' possible. More importantly, this suggests ways young graduates may be conscientious hackers, influencing the built and non-built environment, the real and the virtual, in ways we cannot quite define or describe. It is becoming clear to everyone seduced by the latest advert shown during the Super Bowl that the very software that can help promote, sell and market known architecture today can be the source of new environmental ideas and interactive planning, an up until now unrecognized response to the future.

**[p.u.l.p.**architecture]
**ADVANCED DESIGN**
CRITICS. J.P. Maruszczak, Roger Connah
Spring 2002–04

**We have that choice.**

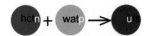

**Urgent:** calling for immediate attention, pressing matters, conveying a sense of urgency, an urge t

laugh, plan, live and change; urgent action; *(arch)* an attempt to map an alternative role fo

architecture and a new approach for the graduate student as an eventual and active professiona

taking on the current confused situation in contemporary architecture and professional engagemen

*(methodology)* an exploration into Urgent poetics, action and the methodologies necessary for future

studies and the disciplines architecture must link with; *(activism)* the urgent groups, minorities an

forces that may need architecture to reform their own conditions; *(model)* an interactive mode

exploring ways in which architecture could re-shape the future; *(question)* when did architects los

the urge for social change, for reform? *(discovery)* of the structures for a renewed dialogue c

architectural factors; *(ethics)* the responsibility, even reckless hope for improvement and socia

change; *(information)* not belligerent resistance but generous risk; *(modelling)* beyond cool, beyon

the rhetoric of slick imaging tools, aiming for a new interactivity; *(mapping)* outliving the trash an

metrodanse of datatowns; *(manifestoi)* an engaged urgent approach (not to be confused with th

urgency of utopian schemes) in the new century as design culture has all but designed itself ou

*(scripts)* beyond prescribed architecture, beyond the continuation of what is already known, more o

less competent, more or less brilliant *(strategies)* necessary for both the profession and active group

within schools, cities and countries; *(motto)* don't respond lightly, strategize and loot *(ecologies)* citie

encountering and re-shaping familiar but urgent ecologies from the lost 'reservation' to th

metaphorical 'desert' to the historical 'beach' *(profession)* review of the power and manipulation of th

architectural brief; *(slang)* pulping, googling, slashing, looting *(gaming)* the subversion of architectura

complacency into game strategy *(now)* here and…

default Planning - the In/site of  Arlington

# the

partial destinies, liminal architectures

# urgent

the conditions of a future unknown - the blue Orange

# studio

# arlington
# we
# have
# a
# problem!

dark departures

knowtopia

the urgent wheel

**[studio**.architecture**]**
**ADVANCED DESIGN**
CRITICS. J.P. Maruszczak, Roger Connah
Spring 2002

u/s

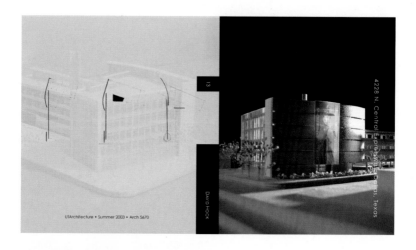

13

4228 N. Central Expressway, Dallas, Texas

David Hock

UTArchitecture • Summer 2003 • Arch 5670

23

Mathias Kapel

architecture 5670
design and sustainability

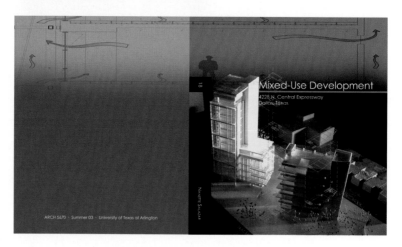

18

Mixed-Use Development

4228 N. Central Expressway
Dallas, Texas

Nanette Salazar

ARCH 5670 • Summer 03 • University of Texas at Arlington

# ADVANCED DESIGN

Advanced Design Studios emphasize the analysis and design of building aggregations within the urban context and the generation and subsequent development of architectural ideas in buildings. Students have the opportunity to select both a studio project and instructor outside of a fixed sequence. Studio projects range in scale, design strategy and approach.

**[studio.architecture]**
**ADVANCED DESIGN**
CRITICS. Jane Ahrens, Richard Ferrier
Summer 2003

STUDENTS. David Hook, Matthias Kafel, Nanette Salazar

# WIENER FAMILY FUND
mountain **HUT** competition

SITE PLAN

FLOOR PLAN 01

FLOOR PLAN 02

1. ENTRY LOBBY
2. CHECK-IN
3. OPEN LOCKERS
4. WORKSHOP / EQUIPMENT RENTAL
5. RESTROOMS / SHOWERS
6. COFFEE SHOP
7. LOUNGE
8. OUTDOOR ROOM
9. COMMONS / SLEEPING QUARTERS

9. OUTDOOR ROOM
10. MORNING DINING
11. VENDING MACHINES
12. FOOD SERVICE
13. KITCHEN
14. EVENING DINING
15. PRIVATE SLEEPING HUTS

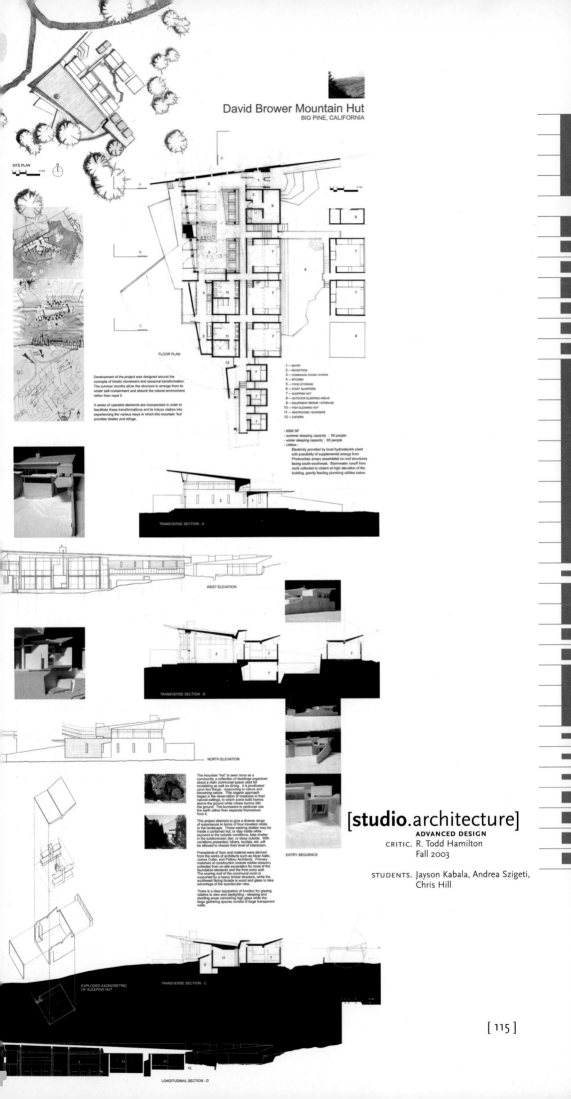

# David Brower Mountain Hut
## BIG PINE, CALIFORNIA

SITE PLAN

FLOOR PLAN

Development of the project was designed around the concepts of kinetic movement and seasonal transformation. The summer months allow the structure to emerge from its winter self-containment and absorb the natural environment rather than repel it.

A series of operable elements are incorporated in order to fascilitate these transformations and to induce visitors into experiencing the various ways in which this mountain 'hut' provides shelter and refuge.

1 – ENTRY
2 – RECEPTION
3 – COMMUNAL ROOM / DINING
4 – KITCHEN
5 – FOOD STORAGE
6 – STAFF QUARTERS
7 – SLEEPING HUT
8 – OUTDOOR SLEEPING AREAS
9 – EQUIPMENT REPAIR / STORAGE
10 – FISH CLEANING HUT
11 – RESTROOMS / SHOWERS
12 – CISTERN

- 6500 SF
- summer sleeping capacity : 90 people
- winter sleeping capacity : 65 people
- Utilities :
    Electricity provided by local hydroelectric plant with possibility of supplemental energy from Photovoltaic arrays assembled on roof structures facing south-southwest. Stormwater runoff from roofs collected in cistern at high elevation of the building, gravity feeding plumbing utilities below.

TRANSVERSE SECTION - A

WEST ELEVATION

TRANSVERSE SECTION - B

NORTH ELEVATION

The mountain "hut" is seen more as a community, a collection of dwellings organized about a main communal space used for socializing as well as dining. It is predicated upon two things: responding to nature and becoming nature. This organic approach began in the observation of creatures in their natural settings, in which some build homes above the ground while others burrow into the ground. The burrowers in particular use the earth rather than separate themselves from it.

This project attempts to give a diverse range of experiences in terms of how travelers relate to the landscape. Those seeking shelter may be inside a contained hut, or stay inside while exposed to the outside conditions, take shelter in the subterranean den, or sleep outside. With variations presented, hikers, tourists, etc. will be allowed to choose their level of interaction.

Precedents of form and material were derived from the works of architects such as Alvar Aalto, James Cutler, and Patkau Architects. Primary materials of construction include rubble masonry collected from on-site excavation for most of the foundation elements and the front entry wall. The soaring roof of the communal room is supported by a heavy timber structure, while the southwest facing facade is wood and glass to take advantage of the spectacular view.

There is a clear separation of function for glazing relative to view and daylighting - sleeping and dwelling areas containing high glass while the large gathering spaces consist of large transparent walls.

ENTRY SEQUENCE

# [studio.architecture]
## ADVANCED DESIGN
CRITIC. R. Todd Hamilton
Fall 2003

STUDENTS. Jayson Kabala, Andrea Szigeti, Chris Hill

EXPLODED AXONOMETRIC OF SLEEPING HUT

TRANSVERSE SECTION - C

LONGITUDINAL SECTION - D

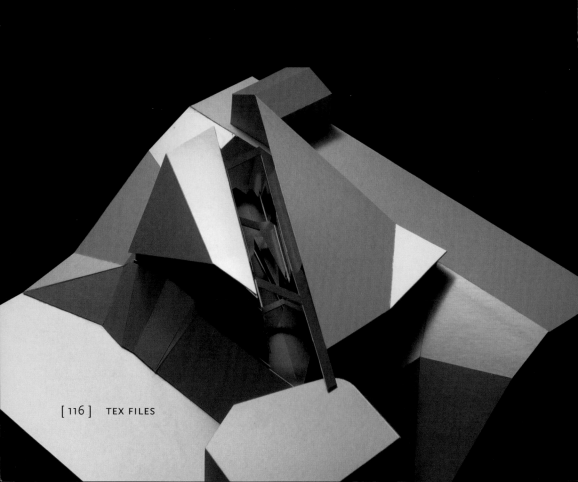

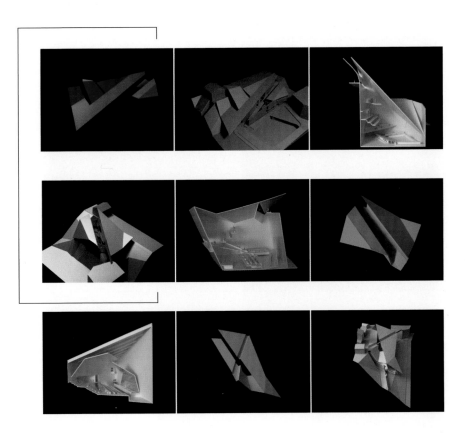

LIFTING A PARLIMENT INTO THE SKY AND PULLING IT DOWN
INTO THE GROUND FOR ANDORRA.

## [**studio**.architecture]
**ADVANCED DESIGN**

CRITIC. Martin Price
Fall 2003

STUDENTS. Jason Hanson
Amanda Fischer
D'jelma Perkison

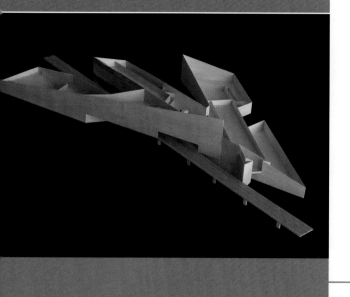

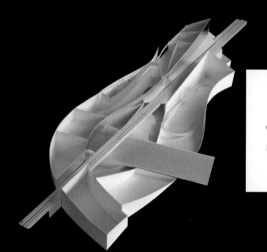

GRAFTING A COMMUNITY CENTER ONTO A
DALLAS DART LIGHT RAIL STATION

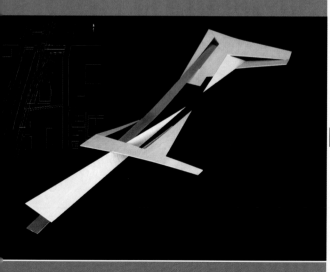

# [studio.architecture]
### ADVANCED DESIGN
CRITIC. Martin Price
Fall 2003

STUDENTS. Amanda Fischer, John Campos,
Matt Wilson, Keith Cummins,
David Birt, Komsorn Khamthiang

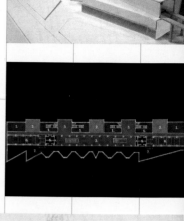

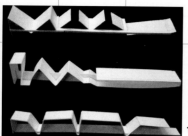

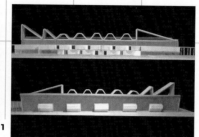

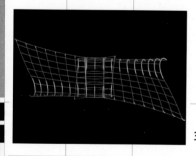

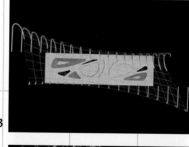

**a provisional theory of architecture**

The **anthropomorphic** (that is to say bodily or literal) inhabitation of a site is less important than one's isomorphic inhabitation of a site. This is not to say that the prosaic is unimportant, only that the day to day requirements of a builder's life, when arbitrarily imposed, are prone to produce **abandonment**.

"This little theory is tentative and **could be abandoned** at any time. **Theories**, like things (and places) are also abandoned. Vanished theories compose the strata of many forgotten books."

—*Robert Smithson* 2

**isomorphism** 1*a*. similarity of different organisms resulting from convergence. 1*b*. similarity of crystalline form between chemical compounds. 2. a one to one correspondence between two mathematical sets, especially a homomorphism that is one to one—**compare endomorphism**—**a mapping of a mathematical set** (as a group, ring, or vector space) into or onto another set or itself in such a way that the result obtained by applying the operations to elements of the first set is mapped onto the result obtained by applying the corresponding operations to their respective images in the second set.

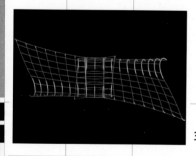

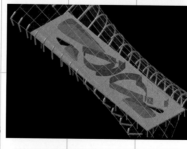

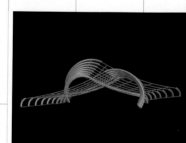

3

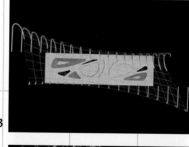

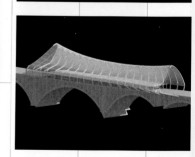

InfoBox project
*student / site*
1 Saul Sloan / Chicago
2 Bradley Bryant / Dallas (+text)
3 Min Jiu Park / Fort Worth
4 Wen Fei Guo / Fort Worth

3

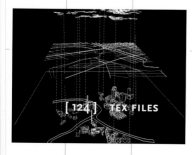

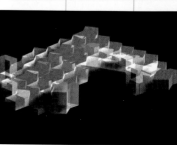

4

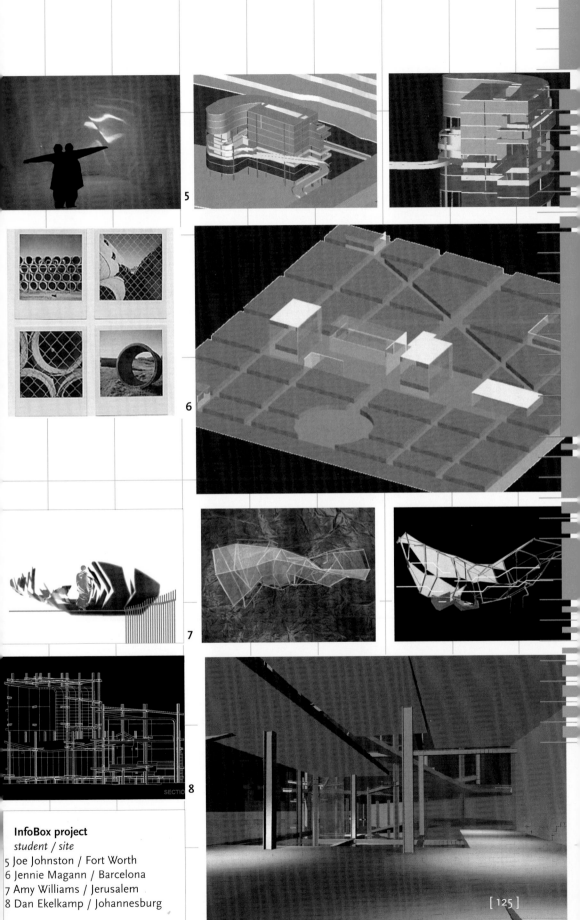

**InfoBox project**
*student / site*
5 Joe Johnston / Fort Worth
6 Jennie Magann / Barcelona
7 Amy Williams / Jerusalem
8 Dan Ekelkamp / Johannesburg

[ 125 ]

9

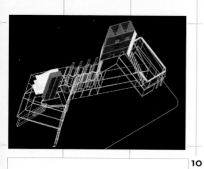

10

**InfoBox project**
*student / site*

9   Troy Brown / Dallas
10  Harshad Pillai / Dallas
11  Chethan Patel / Riyadh
12  Jonathan Bethune / Dallas

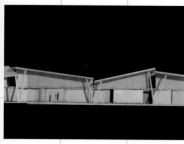

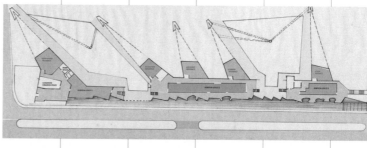

11

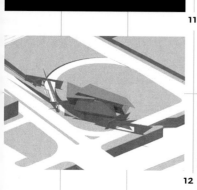

12

[ 126 ]

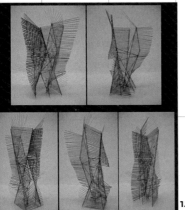

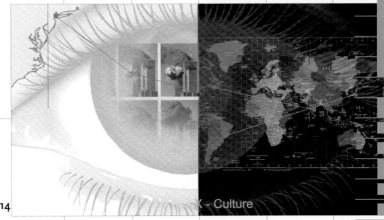

X - Culture

14

15

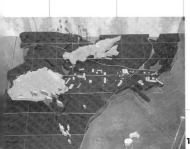

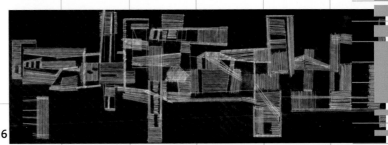

16

17

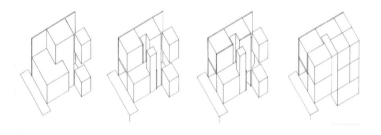

## PATH A

Path A consists of an intensive four semester studio sequence that introduces architectonic theory and operations to students entering the Graduate Program with degrees outside of Architecture. Initial emphasis in Design Studio I is placed on analytic, conceptual, and manipulation procedures while the second semester, Design Studio II, underscores the interrelationship of formal and spatial ideas, use, and the building fabric. These themes continue in Design Studio III with special attention to the urban context. The sequence ends with Design Studio IV which explores complex building designs in urban environments.

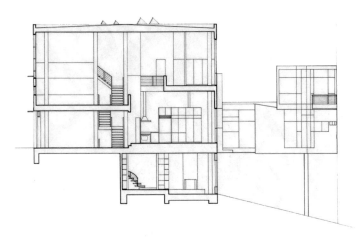

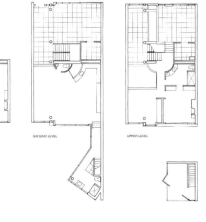

GROUND LEVEL          UPPER LEVEL

# [studio.architecture]
### PATH A: DESIGN STUDIO II
CRITIC. George Gintole
Fall 2002

STUDENT. Dan Eckelkamp

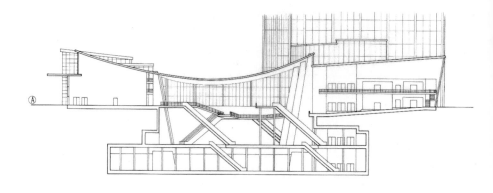

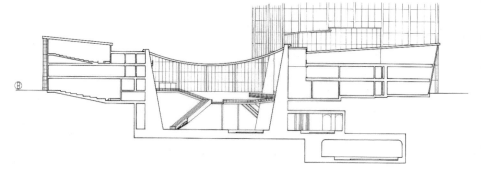

**Future of New York?**

Students analyzed the existing open spaces in New York City—networks, streets, avenues, plazas, parks, and the waterfront. They examined the seven proposals for the *World Trade Center* by the nations' leading architects and put forward their own solution. Emphasis was placed on the correspondence of program, space, scale and time. In the second project, *Designing the Highline*, students entered a New York City competition to redesign, preserve and revise the 22-block-long High Line elevated rail structure.

# [**studio**.architecture]
### PATH A: DESIGN STUDIO III
CRITIC. Karen Bullis
Spring 2003

STUDENTS. Dan Eckelcamp, Peter Pickelman, Eugene Kucej

Holly Arthur, Jury Selection Citation,
Designing the Highline Competition, 2003

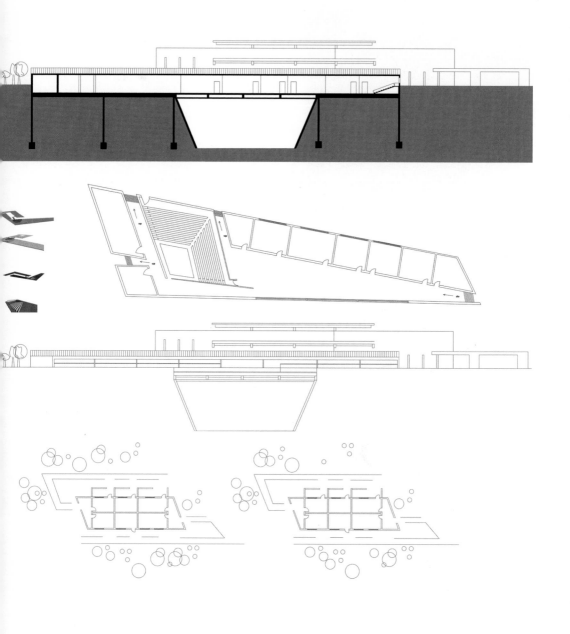

## [**studio**.architecture]
**PATH A: DESIGN STUDIO IV**
CRITIC. Rebecca Boles
Summer 2003

STUDENT. Edyta Skowrou

# The Cultivation of Site

## Landscape Approaches in the Teaching of Urbanism

JESSIE MARSHALL

Shimmering against the bright sky, Donald Judd's huge concrete boxes, cast in the open plain at Marfa, seem to determine the Texas horizon. The rhythm of the boxes—human height, with black shadows thrown hard against shocking sun—alters the perception of field and sky, inscribing a walking pace of passage onto the expansive openness. Reflective, layered, and measured experience of place is conveyed with powerful specificity. Recently arrived from Europe, lost in both the Texas plains and the suburban endlessness of Dallas, I recognized here a rhythm in the desert landscape.

Texas architectural education retains a strong legacy from Colin Rowe. The curricular framework, developed from the influential 1954 University of Texas discourse on space and structure, is condensed in the teaching studio through compositional lessons from collage and analytic cubism—solid and void, balance and juxtaposition—creating a language of architectural abstraction. Within that teaching approach, "the appreciation or precedent of object or figure is assumed to require the presence of some sort of ground field."[i] Furthermore, according to Rowe and Fred Koetter,

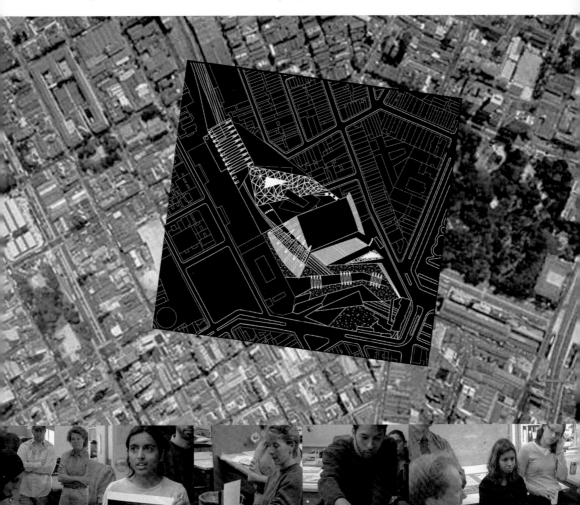

"when figure is unsupported by any recognizable frame of reference, it can only become enfeebled and self-destructive."[ii] Problematically, suburban and open Texas landscapes share a loose fluidity in which "horizontal flow, the horizontal organization of movement is preferred."[iii] In Dallas, extreme suburban blandness and the flat open landscape make evident a lack of traditional urban topographical structure that would ordinarily provide a frame of reference.

How can students of architecture learn to position new works in this context such that their interventions will neither stand in aggressive contrast to, nor disappear into, the given, but participate with it?

Traditional city fabric provides a patchwork structure into which new works can be inserted. Without such a framework, sculptural forms are left floating in their parking lots. One possible approach to positioning architecture in such a context—the enunciation of hidden landscape orders—is revealed in Judd's precise and spare negotiation between body, land, and sky.

### Terrain: Landscape in Architectural Education

Landscape thinking, already valued within urban landscape practice, has become a method through which I teach architecture. Students produce work that settles between fields: landscape orders within urban settings, into which architecture is positioned.[iv] Last year, in a collaborative architecture/landscape-architecture studio at the University of Texas at Arlington, we explored the potential of applying "landscape thinking"—or, more accurately, a diagrammatic thinking developed from landscape theory—to larger urban landscapes, along the way struggling to use GIS as a generative mapping tool. The work was specific to a site in Sao Paulo, Brazil,[v] with its particular social and ecological challenges.

In this essay, I discuss some of the potentials I find in using a deep physical and cultural understanding of contemporary landscape and landscape theory as a strategic framework for the teaching and practice of urban and architectural design. I illustrate these observations with studio projects in which a landscape approach repositioned student thinking about site and architecture.

I propose that a landscape approach to architecture has three main effects. The first is the implicit integration into the work of concerns relevant and important to contemporary urban design practice in its ambitions to revitalize the city. These include ecology and sustainability, time and change both as factors and as design tools, and the large-scale site with local cultural specificities. Such concerns, I propose, are not at all unique to a landscape teaching methodology, merely harder to avoid in

that context. Second, working with a physical landscape necessitates working with maps and engaging with both the potentials and the pitfalls of contemporary mapping methodologies. Here, I refer not only to notational devices for recording topography and time, but to diagrammatic or machinic mapping techniques that reveal and inspire both physical and conceptual content. Aware of the complex conversations that develop around the use of diagrammatic processes, I limit my description to areas of possibility opened up. Third, the physical and perceptual scaling of landscape—that is, of its flexible yet iterative orders—which I discern in Judd's work at Marfa may emerge from the creative processes, revealing specific rhythms and character. While aware of the tenuousness of the idea of "hidden truths" within the landscape, I propose that new orderings of place can emerge, for designers, through the investigative struggle, allowing the designer to come to a specific understanding of place, to cultivate a personal site.

## 1. Grafts: Concerns Appropriated from Landscape

the emphasis on temporality and transformation ... comes in part from landscape design, which has long understood its medium—nature—to be simultaneously dynamic and systemic, and open to interventions that alter the entire system.[vi]

**Spatiality of Time**

The rate at which cities change has increased, and our experience of such change is exaggerated by the pace of life within them. Urban planning always provided a framework for growth, but contemporary plans must celebrate it, with change as an inevitable characteristic. Landscape embodies change. Hence, once described as landscape, it is harder for student projects to be static; plant growth, seasonal change, and fluid uses of infrastructure lead instances into continuities. Calling work landscape is thus partly expedient: it brings issues to the table. Furthermore, landscape works, both drawn and described, articulate changes. Design is not a narrative of static frames viewed over time, but a single diagrammatic function, in which the specificity of each moment can lead to a new, unexpected result.

Large, urban projects need to respond to change, but so do small scale ones. Corporate "hotel-ling," for example, allows no fixed desks. Yet, how can house and city, the loci of our worlds, provide anchors without turning into straight-jackets? Landscape provides three paradigms. First, the calm continuity of environmental change, in daily, seasonal, and geological con-

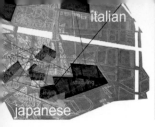

tinuum, provides a model for flow without event. Second, landscape reads functions and motions as integral to the character of place: flows of a site, movements of water, industrial processes, even construction become design factors, with process itself as a building block. Third, we can take advantage of the "re-appearance" of landscape in the cultural sphere. We learn to recognize political process, memory, and local cultural changes as inevitably marked in every landscape, and, through landscape processes, we integrate such fluctuations into the complexity of the mediated object. Again, cultural flows do not engage the reading of site but re-situate themselves as active tools of place-making. James Corner notes the shift from "landscape as a product of culture to landscape as an agent for producing and enriching culture."[vii] In taking on this potential, students discover that change, negotiation, and politics are the stuff from which architecture is made, not obstacles to it.

## Integral Sustainability

Ecological sustainability must be integrated into contemporary cities. If treated as an isolated, quasi-scientific specialization, sustainability leads to simplistic responses through rigid solutions to mechanical problems. In a landscape approach, the ecology of site participates in the full conversation. Student proposals should not be isolated machines for ameliorating climatic problems, but part of a number of situated flows: continuous motions of sun and shadow, water, wind, collection and conservation, weather and decay. These and other flows constitute the panoply of networks layered over a site. Such a model provides a framework for discussion into which we can fold not only geographical networks but local ones as well: vehicular, pedestrian, and social. As a teaching tool, the landscape approach allows radical and vital political issues to be spatialized. As a design tool, it invites integrated thinking with diverse themes in layered juxtaposition.

Landscape ecology ties abstract investigation to local material specificity. Materials and their resistances are powerful teaching tools: their tangible frictions orchestrate a struggle through which design can emerge. Landscape thinking provides a critical framework for such efforts, a structured field for invention.

## Specificity of Place

Even critics of nostalgic postmodern responses to contemporary placelessness still search for ways to conjure up locale. Landscape practices allow particularities of place to emerge, gently and without symbolic frames.

Although it has no more primary claim to regional identity than architecture, landscape may be harder to disassociate from local specificity, and may participate more easily in an evolving cultural milieu.

## 2. Germinations: Mapping Techniques from Landscape

extremely opaque, imaginative, operational instruments ... mappings are neither depictions nor representations, but mental constructs, ideas that enable and effect change.[viii]

The physical techniques of mapping are not, themselves, neutral. Working within landscape practice, one opens teaching procedures to a range of mapping possibilities, with a number of dangers and limits. Clearly, the primary benefit of the map as a notational device is that, through its abstraction, it opens representation to time. Mapping becomes the diagramming not just of data but also of processes, with the potential to reveal not only patterns of use but also patterns of change. The articulation of this gait or "function," in the mathematical sense of that term, is a powerful contribution of landscape methodologies to architectural practices. Like musical notation, however, the map is designed to be experienced through its effects. Here, a certain danger becomes apparent. As already necessarily a visual image, the notation of the mapping itself has a tendency to look like form. Suddenly, the mapping can slide from practice to object: a fixed, idealized, representation. The problem is obvious: imagine if music were suddenly defined as the figure of its notation.

**The Generative Diagram**
Proceeding with halting steps through serial obsessions with form, language, and representation—though, as will be seen, equally with program, force, and performance—the diagram has seemingly emerged as the final tool for architectural production and discourse.[ix]

Creativity in architecture is a complex topic. We find it hard to discuss invention, even in schools ostensibly dedicated to its cultivation. We tend to teach criticism and leave invention to emerge, anxiously. The visible architectural-idea-diagram (e.g., the "parti-diagram" of the 1980s) structured architectural ambition around deeply embedded Classical positions: consistency ostensibly led to clarity, and clarity—like order and balance—were "good." Questioning such fixities, academic use of the diagram eventually changed, taking on new roles: first, as a technique to encourage production; second, as a quasi-scientific, apparently rigorous stage of "site research" before project design; and, third, as a generator of form. Robert

Somol describes a shift in the creative role of diagrams from postwar examples (Rowe/Alexander), which attempted to represent a static truth condition, to more recent uses (Eisenman/Koolhaas) as a method of actively projecting repetition through divergent series.

Landscape mapping in this context can be investigated for its potential to act generatively, as a diagram. This may be both its most powerful and its most problematic role. As a creative tool, mapping ambitiously sponsors the unfolding of imaginative desires and possibilities, what James Corner calls "a theatre of operations." Certainly, strategic mapping practices, such as those discussed above, foster investigation of site with far-reaching potential, provoking creative thinking. However, I differentiate that from the inspirational, "diagrammatic" role of mapping, described by Deleuze as "a catastrophe happening unexpectedly to the canvas, inside figurative or probabilistic data."[x] Deleuze himself made this distinction clear in his assertion that "the diagram is a possibility of fact—it is not the fact itself."[xi] This "chaos,... but also a seed of order," evolves via a figure or technique isolated, momentarily, from place or meaning, providing a catalyst for imaginative play. In this context, we can join Somol in describing diagrammatic work as projective in that it opens new—or, more accurately, virtual—territories for practice.[xii] But teaching must not be tied to specific operational techniques of mapping or folding; these techniques cannot be fixed without losing the very anti-empirical position they attempt to reach. Furthermore, such practices must still struggle to "negotiate the gap between the diagram and the material event."[xiii]

### 3. Conclusion: The Fears of Landscape

As creative tools, methodologies of landscape mapping are typically haunted by at least two fears: that nothing vital of the original map will be preserved in the work and that an anticipated yet hidden truth may not be discovered. They are also often burdened by a secret anxiety that the methodology was just a "getting going," irrelevant to the project itself. Those fears are grounded in the idea of isolated stages in a design process, with landscape mapping as a "research phase" and a wide, difficult gap between that and the design phase. However, if we define the landscape itself as our discourse, then both mappings and design proposals can be seen as continuous iterative stages of the same work. The gap need not be bridged, because it no longer exists. A search for such continuity can be recognized, for example, in emerging work at the Architectural Association, London, in which active mapping practices participate in a strategic process "of systemic idealization and breeding over time.... [The work] is not preconceived

as an ideal but generated as a potential."[xiv] Thus, the mapped work is temporarily articulated in both architectural practice and landscape discourse: it is never completed.

In Texas, my architecture students try to design a landscape. Patterns are discovered and created, emerging from hidden orders of the full environment: topographies, infrastructures, ecologies, histories, even memories and perceptual knowings of site, perhaps invisible but certainly real. These patterns constitute a net—neither geometric, nor historic, but a fabric generated from the land. The design of this fabric is the primary topic of the studio. Into its order, a building project is placed, carefully designed and detailed with the architectural tools at our disposal: material, program, change. The building might be drawn alone but will be the first of an unending sequence, hinting at its continuity, just as the first few steps can hint at the order of a dance. Like Judd's boxes, it will change the pace of the walker and his or her view of the horizon, both revealing the existing landscape and altering our confidence and pace in the experience of it.

NOTES

i    Colin Rowe and Fred Koetter, *Collage City* (Cambridge, Mass.: MIT Press, 1978), 64.

ii   Ibid.

iii  J.B. Jackson, "The Love of Horizontal Spaces," *Discovering the Vernacular Landscape* (New Haven, Conn.: Yale University Press, 1984), 70.

iv   Recently at University of Texas, Arlington, and previously at Cambridge, UK, and Chinese University, Hong Kong.

v    Working with Carlos Leite, Mackenzie University, Sao Paulo, Brazil.

vi   Detlef Mertins, "landscapeurbanismhappensintime," in *Landscape Urbanism* (London: Architectural Association, 2003), 135.

vii  James Corner, "Introduction," *Recovering Landscape* (New York: Princeton Architectural Press, 1999), 4.

viii James Corner, "The Agency of Mapping," *Mappings*, ed. Denis Cosgrove (London: Reaktion Press, 1999), 250.

ix   Robert Somol, "Dummy Text, or the Diagrammatic Basis of Contemporary Architecture," in *Peter Eisenman, Diagram Diaries* (New York: Universe Books (Rizzoli), 1999), 7.

x    Gilles Deleuze, "The Diagram," *The Deleuze Reader*, ed. Constantin Boundas (New York: Columbia University Press, 1993), 194.

xi   Ibid, 199.

xii  Somol, "Dummy Text," 24.

xiii Andrew Benjamin, AA lecture series, 2004.

xiv  Ciro Najle, "Plan," in *Landscape Urbanism* (London: Architectural Association, 2003), 119. The work described at the AA takes place in Najle's Landscape Urbanism studio, which is illustrated in the book.

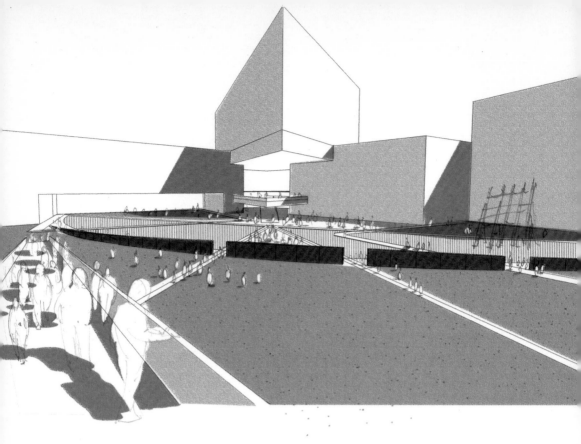

# [studio.landscape]
**ADVANCED DESIGN**
World Trade Center Memorial
Summer 2003

STUDENTS. Amy Archambeau, Jeff Hsiao, Hsing-Yeh Ho

# Rebirth and Renaissance

## The Aftermath of Tragedy

### Reflecting on the Past

Nature provides a path toward transcending fear and painful memories of the past. These reflections are not to be avoided; confronting them is an important part of the healing process. The design encourages the visitor to ponder, meditate, and ultimately accept what happened at this historic place.

### Reliving and Putting to Rest

The design highlights the historical significance of the site as an arena where a critical event occurred—an event serving as a fulcrum upon the American psyche has turned it in a new direction. At the site nature offers, through its beauty, uplifting and powerful visual experiences to the visitor. The design does not suppress tragic memories—it recalls and mirrors site-specific images.

### Regaining Perspective on Continuing Life

The site provides an opportunity to celebrate life, unite humanity, and regain hope for the future. The experience is a reminder that the life force prevails, even in the face of catastrophe.

### Refreshing the Spirit

Water within a public space inevitably draws people to it. The water is emblematic of the manner in which the human family has been drawn together by the tragedy of the site, and how the human family will heal itself by coming together there.

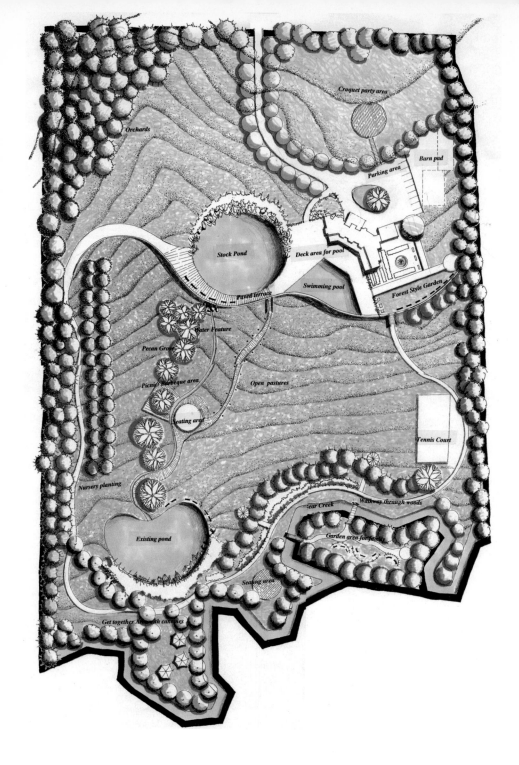

Orchards

Croquet party area

Barn pad

Parking area

Stock Pond

Deck area for pool

Swimming pool

Paved terrace

Forest Style Garden

Water Feature

Pecan Grove

Open pastures

Picnic Barbeque area

Seating area

Tennis Court

Nursery planting

Clear Creek

Walkway through woods

Existing pond

Garden area for family

Seating area

Get together Area with canopies

# [**studio**.landscape]
### ADVANCED DESIGN
CRITIC. David Hopman
Fall 2003

STUDENTS. Biff Sturgess, Priti Ramanujam

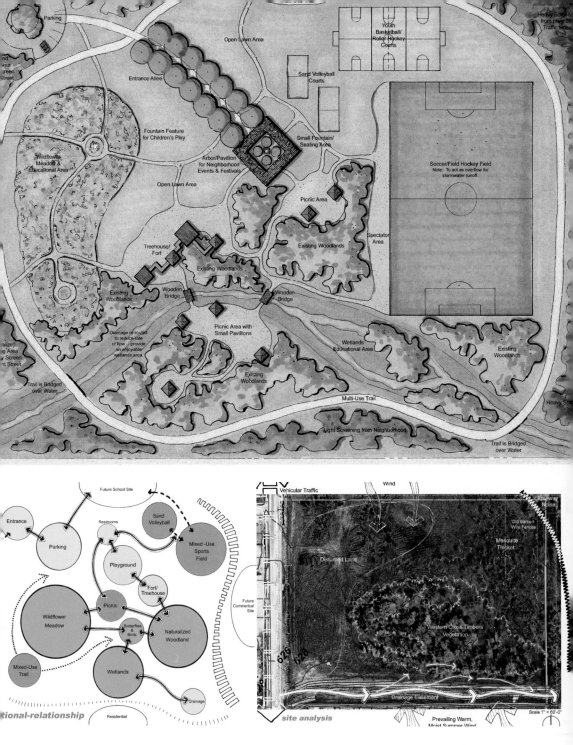

# Featured  >

Fort Worth, Texas

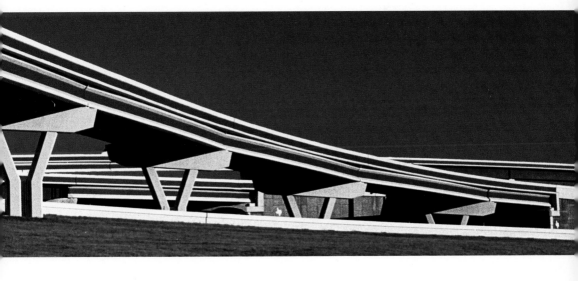

# Écriture

# Writing (*Riding*) in a Culture of Images

GEORGE GINTOLE

Images expressed by various means of scribing are intriguing and considered unique as they are often examined individually. These forms of text and image isolate themselves by virtue of their expressive style, yet each mark or transgression may lend itself to a broad and more encompassing spectrum of philosophical, cultural, or artistic contexts. The French word *écriture,* coined by the philosopher Roland Barthes, has no direct English translation. Écriture doesn't embody a univalent notion or act (its closest English translation is "scripture," but that bears much more direct references). More generally écriture, or "writings," as Barthes often uses, relies on a special inflection or tone, an ethos or "spirit of a culture."

Analogical parallels are drawn as we examine the act of scribing from three categories of scribes on multiple scales with a variety of instruments and surfaces. The first of the scribe categories includes artists as farmers or farmers as artists whose transgressions find their way on the landscape (the riders). These land artists of today, who often work in the same media as farmers, take full advantage of modern farm technology, using tractor- drawn tools, fertilizer, and even fire as instruments of their craft. The second category is comprised of contemporary calligraphers in both the Eastern and Western hemispheres. This particular group, like those working on the landscape, is also constantly searching for new instruments with which to create using tools fashioned from landscape elements as well as fire and water. Finally, the third group of scribes includes subway artists, who refer to themselves as "writers." The direct parallel between "scribing" the earth, the calligrapher's scribing, and the "writing" on subway walls is all écriture and a question of scale.

In the reading of these acts, the mind first focuses on the materiality of the image of interest, after which we read its denotative power and its direct ability to describe objects or words. The connotative potential of the image to refer to philosophical, political, cultural, or artistic contexts is where the emphasis is placed.

While the emphemeral quality of the land art projects has its roots in the 1970s escape from gallery walls propelled by artists like Michael Heizer and Robert Smithson, its temporality introduced real time as a coordinate. The idea of "art as event" or "art as experience" has its urban parallel with the graffiti artists, who had to "write" in limited space between parked subway cars and had to leave their marks before the police arrived. It is by virtue of the camera as a recording instrument that these "acts of transgression" actually transcend their temporality—the photograph stamps it with its own relative permanence.

[featured.faculty]

CRITIC. George Gintole

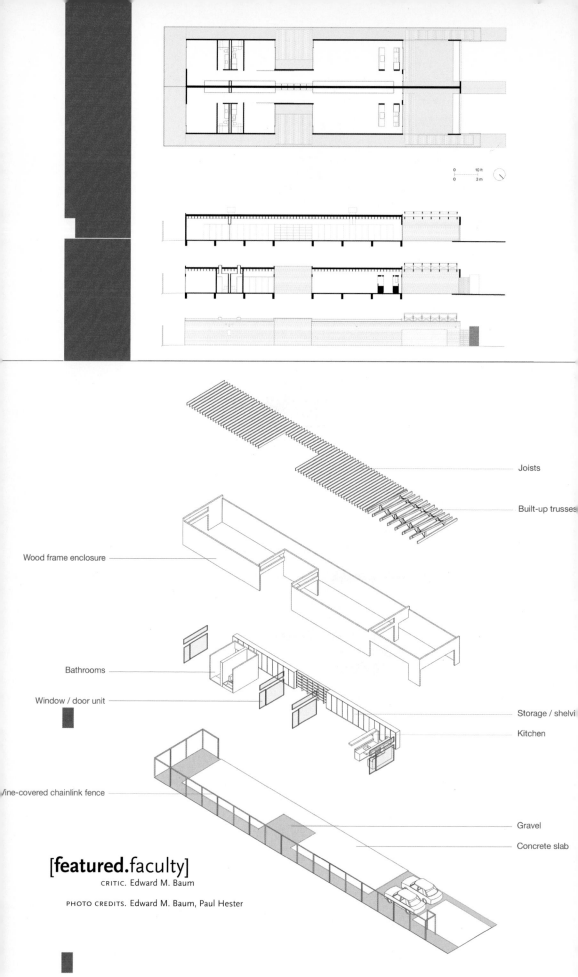

Joists

Built-up trusses

Wood frame enclosure

Bathrooms

Window / door unit

Storage / shelvi

Kitchen

Vine-covered chainlink fence

Gravel

Concrete slab

# [featured.faculty]

CRITIC. Edward M. Baum

PHOTO CREDITS. Edward M. Baum, Paul Hester

## Commemorative Design

To commemorate the employees who lost their lives on September 11, 2001, American Airlines contacted VLK Architects to design a memorial. Architecture intern and 2002 graduate of UT Arlington School of Architecture, Stephanie Cross was selected to design the plaque.

Constructed of stainless steel and black granite, the memorial stands three feet four inches tall and is located at the American Airlines Flight Academy in Fort Worth, Texas. It is dedicated to the employees of American Airlines who lost their lives on September 11, 2001.

In the category Details-Furniture-Graphics of the 2002 Excellence in Architecture Awards, sponsored by the Fort Worth Chapter of the American Institute of Architects, the American Airlines September 11th Memorial earned a merit award.

"It was always [because of] the words of encouragement from both of my parents that I remained confident in my abilities as an individual and as an artist," Cross says.

Cross also credits professors George Gintole and John Maruszczak with influencing her to engage design with both sensibility and energy. "After taking the first architecture studio with Professor Gintole and the second with Maruszczak I had found the love of my life—architecture."

Location: Fort Worth, Texas

Client-Owner: American Airlines

Contractors:
Sigma Granite & Marble
Volume Millwork, Inc.
Thos. S. Byrne, Inc.

MARY JANE "M.J."
EDDIE DILLARD
CAPTAIN WILSON "B
DARLENE "DEE" FL

dyn**a**mic

fo**r**m,

structure, symphony, r h y t h m, stoic, **passion**.

As memories mark time,

fo**ot**s**t**eps, the tangible existence,

character the individual essence of life,

life becomes a form.

a form of layers, process, that can

be seen through MINDS, CHAOS, BEGINNING & END.

this process in itself recalls, in its form,

the act of memory & it's relationship

to the built form.

And it is with details that architecture
is realized and formed.

it is in our finest perception of CONCEPT
and our ideas behind design that

precision, form, rhythm and scale

create po**e**try.

MERIT

AWARD

AIA FORT WORTH

2002 EXCELLENCE IN ARCHITECTURE AWARDS

Gin or Vodka?   **Gin**
Dog or Cat?   **Dog**
Greatest Indulgence?
              **Travelling, time off**
Mies or Corb?   **Corb**
Ghery or Zumthor?
              **Zumthor**
New York or LA?   **NY**
Turkey burger or beef?   **Beef**
Flush detail or overlay?
              **Flush**
BW or color?   **BW**
Buffet or Taylor?   **Taylor**
Letterman or Leno?
              **Letterman**
If your practice was
              somewhere else
              besides Dallas
              where would it be?
              **Europe**

**[featured**.alumnus**]**

Jennie Magann

## Observations from an Intern

Sharon Odum has been a licensed architect for 14 years and has won several AIA awards. She received her undergraduate education from UT Arlington and attended Rice University for graduate studies. She started out working for Omniplan, a large firm where she worked a couple of years before deciding to go back to graduate school. Sharon eventually ended up in a small firm working with Gary Cunningham. Recently, she decided to start her own practice, *Sharon Odum Architect*.

Sharon is an army of one —plus me. Her practice operates out of an office owned by Gary Cunningham who sublets to other professionals. The office is much like a studio in that the desks are messy, there is a complete wood shop in the back, and at least one of us is covered in sawdust and grease. People often borrow tools, books, and music from each other, and there is always someone begging for chocolate.

My general duties so far have been anything but mundane. They range from marking shop drawings and submittals—often in Sharon's car on the way to the site—cutting metal pipe in Gary's shop, building models, picking up lunch, ordering samples, returning phone calls, some design schematic, cad drawings, brochure layout, and keeping Sharon's coffee cup full—not on her request, simply because she needs it. I never know what is coming and every day is different.

You can always find Sharon at the coolest lectures, gallery openings, Marfa, Texas ... you name it, she's there. She is so accessible, her architecture is accessible and she doesn't sugar coat conversation or cloud ideas. Her clear articulation is expressed in her personality as well as her design.